Battle Orders • 35

Panzer Divisions: The Eastern Front 1941–43

Pier Paolo Battistelli

Consultant editor Dr Duncan Anderson • *Series editors* Marcus Cowper and Nikolai Bogdanovic

First published in Great Britain in 2008 by Osprey Publishing, Midland House, West Way, Botley, Oxford OX2 0PH, United Kingdom.
Email: info@ospreypublishing.com

ISBN-13: 978 1 84603 338 4

Editorial by Ilios Publishing, Oxford, UK (www.iliospublishing.com)
Page layout by Bounford.com, Cambridge, UK
Maps by Bounford.com, Cambridge, UK
Typeset in Monotype Gill Sans and ITC Stone Serif
Index by Sandra Shotter
Originated by United Graphics Pte
Printed and bound in China through Bookbuilders

08 09   10 9 8 7 6 5 4 3 2 1

A CIP catalogue record for this book is available from the British Library.

For a catalogue of all books published by Osprey Military and Aviation please contact:

Osprey Direct USA, c/o Random House Distribution Center, 400 Hahn Rd, Westminster, MD 21157 USA
E-mail: info@ospreydirect.com

Osprey Direct UK, P.O. Box 140, Wellingborough, Northants, NN8 2FA, UK
E-mail: info@ospreydirect.co.uk

www.ospreypublishing.com

Acknowledgements

The author wishes to thank the following people for their help: Nik Cornish, Antonio Attarantato and Carlo Pecchi for the photographs; Mr Andrew Orgill and the staff of the Central Library, Royal Military Academy Sandhurst; Dr Christopher Pugsley and Dr Klaus Schmider (Department of War Studies, Royal Military Academy Sandhurst) for their friendly help and support and, last but not least, the series editors Marcus Cowper and Nikolai Bogdanovic.

Author's note

In the tree diagrams and maps in this volume, the units and movements of national forces are depicted in the following colours:

German units   Grey
Soviet units   Red

German number and case endings are often omitted in the text for clarity and to avoid confusion for readers.

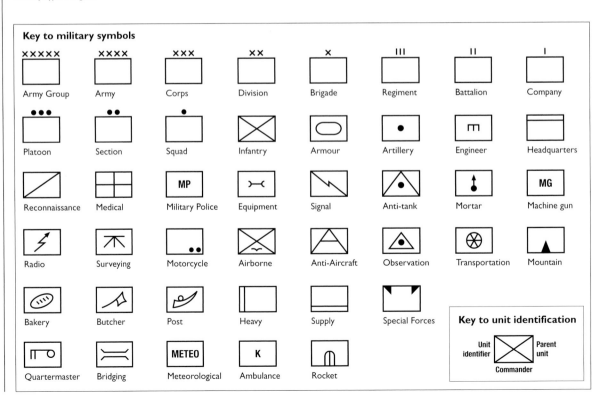

Contents

Introduction

Blitzkrieg unleashed on the Eastern Front: Panzer Regiment 35 from 4. Panzer Division deploys to attack the town of Sluzk, 26 June 1941. In the foreground stands an SdKfz 253 artillery observation vehicle.

On 22 June 1941, when Operation *Barbarossa* was unleashed, there was no longer any doubt; the Panzerwaffe, the German armoured branch, was the new, decisive instrument of modern land warfare – and it would be the tool that Germany would use to overcome her enemies. In the wake of the fall of France and the German victory in the West in June 1940, Hitler ordered the doubling of the number of Panzer and motorized infantry divisions, seeking a new, larger and better-mechanized army. The months before *Barbarossa* clearly shown how correct his desire had been; in April the German Army, spearheaded by its Panzer Divisions, quickly conquered both Yugoslavia and Greece, while in North Africa, Rommel's Panzers reconquered all of the territory – except Tobruk – that the Italians had lost the previous winter. In the first weeks of *Barbarossa*, it appeared that the war on the Eastern Front was going to follow the same pattern as the Panzer Divisions, spearheading the German forces, drove deep into Soviet territory, encircling large numbers of Red Army units. The extent of these initial successes was such that in early July 1941 an overconfident General Franz Halder, chief of staff of the German Army, wrote in his diary that the war against the Soviet Union had been won. Events would prove that Halder was quite wrong.

Two years later, having survived two massive defeats, the German Army once again stood ready to attack on the Eastern Front, led by its Panzer Divisions. This time, however, the setting was completely different; the main purpose of this new offensive was to regain the initiative and, unlike the two previous summers, no one was thinking any longer of blitzkrieg. The eventual failure of this 1943 attack (Operation *Zitadelle*) – which was doomed even before it began – simply marked the end of a long process that had started with *Barbarossa*. It was a process that saw the Panzer Divisions – as well as modern, mechanized land warfare – endure a series of changes that shaped land warfare in the years to come.

The German successes of 1939–40 had demonstrated that blitzkrieg was possible, yet in 1941 it took fewer than six months to discover that it would not always be so – and the lesson was learned the hard way. Not only would the Soviet Union remain undefeated by blitzkrieg, but when the Red Army struck back, the German Army barely managed to escape disaster. Panzer Divisions suffered such severe losses that what was left of them was nothing more than a mere shadow of the once-triumphant Panzerwaffe. In the wake of this, a reorganization took place, and a new offensive was unleashed. However, there was little resemblance now to the blitzkrieg-style warfare of the previous years. Again, in winter 1942/43, the German Army suffered a further major defeat, which the Panzer Divisions were unable to prevent. In early 1943, yet another reorganization took place, and a new offensive was planned. By this time, however, the Panzer Divisions' methods of waging war had been significantly altered. In the light of the failure of *Zitadelle*, the Panzer Divisions appeared a distant shadow of that new, decisive instrument of warfare they had been deemed only three years earlier.

Combat mission

Successfully adapted and tested in the field during the 1940 campaign, the German principles of war provided the basis of the planning of *Barbarossa*. The plan envisaged an in-depth penetration by the Panzergruppe, which was tasked with surrounding and encircling enemy forces, which would then be mopped up by German infantry units. This annihilation of enemy forces was sought by targetting a main *Schwerpunkt* ('centre of gravity'), which would destroy the bulk of Red Army units in the area and split the front in two. Two separate German advances to the north and the south of the main advance were to play only a secondary role until they could be given greater support in the advance to their objectives – Leningrad and the Dniepr River. Since the annihilation of enemy forces was more critical than the seizure of specific targets, no objectives were fixed, save for the seizure of Moscow, which was to mark the last stage of the campaign.

Like the 1940 campaign in the West, *Barbarossa* required the enemy to deploy the bulk of his forces forwards, thus allowing for his encirclement and destruction – a distinct possibility given the poor condition the Red Army found itself in, lacking leadership at every echelon. The speed of advance was essential to the success of blitzkrieg, in order to prevent the Red Army from establishing a firm defensive line. A speedy conclusion to the campaign (which, according to German planners, would be within four to five months) was also desirable, bringing victory before the Soviet Union could fully mobilize its men and resources – a process that the Germans estimated would take a year. While the plan for *Barbarossa* was based on the same premises as the 1940 campaigns – though adapted to a completely different environment – namely the use of speed, manoeuvre and in-depth penetration with the aim of encircling and annihilating the enemy – the operational plan did not, and could not, match that of the 'sickle cut' of 1940.

A group of Soviet prisoners is escorted back to a collection point by an SdKfz 251 during the German offensive of summer 1942. The German officer shielding his eyes from the sun is the Knight's Cross winner Oberst Maximilian von Edersheim, then commanding Panzergrenadier Regiment 26.

The first weeks of *Barbarossa* saw the Panzers make rapid advances and Soviet forces taking heavy losses, outshining the German achievements of 1940. However, problems soon surfaced. The lack of a suitable road network slowed down the German follow-up infantry and supplies, with the result that the Panzers failed to complete the encirclement of the enemy. The infantry took longer than expected to mop up enemy forces and the Panzer Divisions became worn out; to compound matters, the Soviet mobilization came sooner than expected. Autumn, with its unfavourable climate, soon bogged down Operation *Taifun*, the German assault on Moscow. Time and space – two unforeseen factors – took their toll, and eventually the Soviet counter-offensive of December 1941 brought the German Army and the Panzerwaffe face to face with their first defeat, which was to have dire consequences for the Germans.

The German offensive launched in 1942 (aimed not only at the destruction of enemy forces but also at the seizure of the Soviet oil sources) was based on different premises to the previous year. Since the Panzer Divisions had lost much of their edge and now lacked both flexibility and 'penetrating power', Hitler ordered them to closely cooperate with the infantry to avoid gaps in their encirclements. The Panzer Divisions were intermingled with infantry and were dispersed over a wide area, following the decision to split the offensive in two. Moreover, the Soviet withdrawal that followed the beginning of the new offensive completely thwarted any chance of waging blitzkrieg warfare again. As the battles around Kharkov of 1942 and 1943 showed, the Germans were now capable of outmanoeuvring the Red Army only when allowed to do so. Facing its own shortcomings and the growing capabilities of the enemy, the notion of blitzkrieg died; firepower prevailed over speed and manoeuvrability, with the result being that Operation *Zitadelle* would be based on a concept which would have been inconceivable a year earlier: attacking the enemy where it was strongest. Mechanized warfare had entered a new era.

Doctrine and training

Germany's victorious 1940 campaign shaped its armoured warfare doctrine, helping to further refine the tactics of the Panzerwaffe. First, experience gained in difficult terrain such as the wetlands around Dunkerque had shown that the Panzer Divisions needed more infantry and a better balance between armour, infantry and support weapons. This was also demonstrated by the experiences of the 'four tank battalion' brigades, which proved too cumbersome to manoeuvre efficiently. The subsequent reorganization of these units into a single Panzer Regiment was another step forward in German doctrine, which conceived of such a division as an all-arms, balanced unit capable of carrying out every kind of mission by itself. Yet, true to the concept of concentrating their forces, the Germans stressed that the best way in which the Panzer Divisions could be employed was within the Panzerkorps (armoured corps), itself part of the Panzergruppe (armoured army).

Shortly after the conclusion of the 1940 campaign, commanders at every level were requested to submit detailed reports about their own experiences in the field. These were used to improve the 1938 technical manual, which was reissued on 3 December 1940 under the title *Directives for Command and Employment of a Panzer Division (Heeres-Dienstvorschrift g 66)*. It was reprinted in 1942 without further changes, and its guidelines remained unaltered until the end of the war. It stated that the main task of the Panzer Division was to seek decision on the battlefield. A Panzer Division was required to attack every kind of enemy position and to exploit the success using either in-depth penetration behind enemy lines or attacking an enemy's rear positions, and pursuing any enemy remnants. Attack was the only combat method suited to the Panzer Divisions; even in defence they were to counter-attack enemy breakthroughs. Only when facing fixed or fortified defence lines were the Panzer Divisions to give way to the infantry, not only to avoid severe losses but also to avoid eschewing the decisive advantage of their speed and manoeuvrability.

Those dual advantages were the decisive factors in a Panzer Division attack. Tanks no longer ruled the battlefield alone, although they were still the decisive weapon that required concentration – nothing less than a Panzer Abteilung was to be used. Attacking only with tanks meant attacking into a void, while combined arms warfare was the best solution. This required close cooperation between tanks, infantry, artillery and other support units such as engineers and anti-tank units. The classic attack saw Panzer units breaking through and conquering the area with the aid of engineers (who opened the path of advance across obstacles, mines in particular) and supported by artillery fire. Meanwhile, infantry secured the area, mopping up the enemy and defending the flanks. There were several ways in which the Panzers and infantry could cooperate, though initially the preferred one was for mechanized infantry to closely follow up the Panzer attack. Heavy fire and fast movement were the keys to a successful attack. First, suitable terrain had to be chosen (wooded and built-up areas were quite unsuitable); second, while the artillery kept pace with the Panzer and infantry advance, attacking units were to reach their firing positions quickly. Third, as soon as a breakthrough had been made, the enemy forces had to be encircled and attacked in their rear.

Combined-arms warfare led to the widespread use of mixed Kampfgruppen (combat groups), which involved splitting up a Panzer Division into two or more mixed groups. The main combat group consisted of the Panzer Regiment and the armoured Schützen Bataillon plus an Artillerie Abteilung, a company of Pioniere (armoured engineer battalion) and one of Panzerjäger. (What was

The original caption to this photo notes that snow could do little harm to German tanks – though it certainly did to their crews. It shows a line of PzKpfw IIIs on the move during Operation *Taifun*, in autumn 1941.

In mid-September 1942, 3. Panzer Division attacked in the Nogaj steppe just north of the Caucasus Mountains, trying to cut the military supply roads leading south. The attempt failed in the face of formidable Soviet defences. Here a group of Panzergrenadiers advances behind the cover of a PzKpfw III.

Training

Following the reorganization of autumn 1940, there was an injection of new soldiers into the Panzer Divisions. The rank and file became younger, at most 26 years old, and experienced officers and NCOs were transferred to other units while new ones were commissioned from experienced personnel. Training started at the lowest level, taking advantage of the experience gained by battle-tested officers and NCOs in the cadres. However, since doctrine stressed combined-arms warfare, training also took place at divisional level between different units such as Panzer, Schützen and artillery regiments. Particular emphasis was placed on rapid movement and exploitation of circumstances, including in wooded and built-up areas and in conditions of poor visibility, such as at night or in fog. Combined-arms warfare also meant that every unit had to learn how to keep up with the Panzers' pace of advance, in particular the artillery and dismounted infantry. However, the extensive reorganization and restructuring of units and personnel eventually had an effect on divisional-level training, particularly amongst newly formed units. The situation deteriorated after the winter of 1941, when specialist troops (such as Panzer crewmen) were forced to fight as infantry, suffering heavy losses that were hard to replace. Eventually, some divisions had to be withdrawn from the front and sent to Germany or France to reorganize fully.

left of the Schützen Brigade and the artillery, engineers and anti-tank units, plus the Aufklärungs Abteilung, could form one or more groups.) The main group would spearhead the advance, breaking through the enemy defences and heading for its target, leaving the tasks of mopping up and securing conquered areas, or reconnoitring the flanks, to support groups (either moving on the wings or following up). The mixed Kampfgruppen replaced the Panzer and Schützen brigades as the main attack and support groups of the division, though every combat element retained its particular role.

It did not take long before the war on the Eastern Front exposed the shortcomings of German doctrine. The lack of an adequate road network and accurate maps, the erroneous estimates for fuel consumption (60,000 litres of fuel daily for a 200-tank Panzer Regiment soon turned into 120,000 and 180,000 litres daily) and the wear and tear on the vehicles greatly influenced the Panzer Divisions' capabilities, along with the inability of the infantry to keep pace with the armoured advance. Until 27 June 1941 Panzergruppen 2 and 3 advanced 320km with a daily rate of 64km, but this shrank to 20km a day in early July. Likewise, 8. Panzer Division's daily rate of advance was 75km until 26 June, but this dropped to 32km in the first half of July. Autumn brought the first bad weather, and the resulting quagmire, which restricted the Panzer Divisions to movement on the main roads, made manoeuvre and encirclement practically impossible. Winter combined with improvements to the Soviet defences, with their anti-tank guns deployed forward, further reduced the mobility of the Panzer Divisions. Eventually, the severe losses suffered during the first Soviet counter-offensive and the subsequent reorganization of the Panzer Divisions crushed any German hopes of victory.

In 1942 the Panzer Divisions were still an effective fighting force, despite having only part of their established strength. Along with improvements made to the Red Army, this eventually tipped the balance in favour of firepower rather than movement and, in order to spare tanks, German attacks were led more often by the infantry with artillery support. The Panzer was no longer the decisive weapon and was now used rather for support and exploitation, while infantry and artillery were deemed the best weapons for breaking through. The structure of the Kampfgruppe changed accordingly, as more Panzer units were broken down to company level, especially since only one Panzer Abteilung was available. Also, since the Panzerkorps and the Panzergruppe now featured a mixture of Panzer and infantry divisions, the former came to be used as battering rams for breaking through enemy fixed defences.

Although the Panzer Divisions were still capable of manoeuvring and striking in depth, even if to a reduced extent, the rest of the German Army was no longer able to support them in these roles. Eventually, this reshaped the entire notion of armoured warfare, as the doomed Operation *Zitadelle* showed. As a consequence, the Panzer Divisions would soon be entrusted with a new task.

A mixed column, part of an unknown Kampfgruppe, moving to meet the enemy, January 1943. In 1941 the Germans developed the use of mixed 'battle groups' made up of different units. As seen here, they may have included armour, infantry, artillery and other support units such anti-tank and engineer elements.

A PzKpfw 38 (t) hauls a car out of the mud in autumn 1941. With the coming of the *rasputitsy* ('the times without roads') during the heavy rains of autumn and spring, most of the Soviet road network became impassable for non-tracked vehicles, which featured heavily in the Panzer Divisions.

Providing replacements for the Panzer Divisions

Each German Army unit was mobilized in a particular area located in one of the 18 Wehrkreis (military districts) into which Germany and annexed territories were divided. These were part of the Ersatzheer (replacement army) which, amongst other tasks, was in charge of the call-up and training of new recruits, NCOs and officers, and of the training and replacement units. Every combat unit down to battalion level had its own counterpart in the Ersatzheer. Following mobilization, the first unit joined the Feldheer (field army) going to its division or other command, while the latter (made up of cadres) remained in place and was filled with new recruits. For example, 1. Panzer Division was raised in Wehrkreis IX (HQ at Kassel), located in Hessen, part of Thuringia. The home station of the division was Erfurt, and its units were raised in other parts of Thuringia including Weimar, Langensalza and Eisenach. Thus, Schützen Regiment 1 had its Ersatz counterpart in the Schützen Ersatz Bataillon 1 (Weimar); Kradschützen

Bataillon 1 referred to Kradschützen Ersatz Bataillon 1 (Meiningen), while Panzer Regiment 1 referred to the Panzer Ersatz Abteilung 1 (Erfurt), which was made up of the former first and sixth Panzer Kompanie plus the third and seventh Panzer Kompanie from Panzer Regiment 2 (it actually provided replacements for both Panzer Regiments). Trained personnel from every Ersatz (replacement) unit would then create a Marsch Kompanie, eventually forming the Marsch Bataillon, which would be sent to join its parent division. This would see it taken into the Feldersatz Bataillon (field replacement battalion). Here further training and acclimatization followed, until replacement personnel were sent to their final destination.

In October 1942, due to the increased pressures on manpower, most Ersatzheer units were split in two, forming an Ersatz and an Ausbildung (training) battalion. While the former continued to perform its duties with newly called up recruits, the latter – composed of partly trained recruits – was sent outside Germany and used to garrison occupied areas, thus

freeing Feldheer units for the front. Newly called up recruits received basic training with the Ersatz unit, and were then sent to the Ausbildung unit to complete training, eventually joining a Marsch Kompanie being sent to the Feldheer. In early 1943, Heinz Guderian, the newly appointed inspector general of the Panzertruppe, took over the Panzer Divisions' replacement system, creating a Kommandeur der Panzertruppen in every Wehrkreis to directly control replacements and schools. In April four Reserve Panzer Divisions, actually made up of a few Ausbildung units, were created, followed by a fifth in November. These were sent either to France (155, 178, 179 and 273. Reserve Panzer Divisions) or Denmark (233. Reserve Panzer Division), and eventually were used to replenish any badly mauled Panzer Divisions. In May 1944, 155. Reserve Panzer Division was absorbed by 9. Panzer Division, 179. Reserve Panzer Division was used to create 116. Panzer Division and 273. Reserve Panzer Division was absorbed by 11. Panzer Division.

Unit organization

Reorganizing the Panzer Divisions

Even before the end of the campaign in the West, the Oberkommando des Heeres (OKH, Army High Command) started to plan a reorganization of armoured and motorized divisions. The first figure of 24 Panzer and 12 motorized infantry divisions drafted at the end of May 1940 was reduced by mid-June to 20 Panzer and 10 motorized infantry divisions, though in April 1941 a new plan for the post-*Barbarossa* army envisaged the creation by the following autumn of another four to six new Panzer Divisions, four of which were actually formed during the year. Although no overall establishment was laid down, the reorganization of the ten old Panzer Divisions and the creation of ten new ones followed the guidelines dictated by the experiences made during the campaign in the West, in addition to an attempt to obtain uniformity. As a result, every Panzer Division now had one two-battalion Panzer Regiment (the old 1–3, 4, 5 and 10. Panzer Divisions lost one); one Schützen Brigade with two regiments, each with two battalions (1–3, 6–8. Panzer

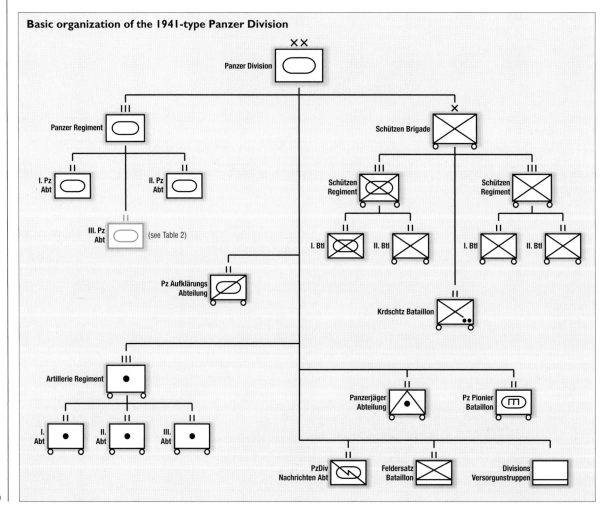

Basic organization of the 1941-type Panzer Division

Divisions formed a second Schützen Regiment using their third battalions), plus a Kradschützen Bataillon (4, 5 and 10. Panzer Divisions formed a new one) and a three-battalion Artillerie Regiment which, in the old Panzer Divisions, simply led to the permanent attachment of the Artillerie Abteilung already available before May 1940. As before, every division also included a reconnaissance unit (Panzer Aufklärungs Abteilung), anti-tank (Panzerjäger Abteilung), engineer (Pionier Bataillon) and communications units (Nachrichten Abteilung), plus a field replacement battalion and divisional supply and service units.

However, complete uniformity was not attained. By June 1941 four Panzer Divisions still retained the Panzer Brigade Stab (HQ), Panzer Regiments had either two or three Abteilungen and six divisions had a schwere Infanterie Geschütz Kompanie (heavy infantry gun company) attached to their Schützen Brigade (see Table 1 on page 12). Heavy losses suffered during winter 1941/42 and the subsequent reorganization of those Panzer Divisions scheduled to take part in the new summer offensive brought new changes, mainly affecting the number of Panzer Abteilungen in the Panzer Regiment. Also the Panzer Aufklärungs Abteilung was disbanded and merged with the Kradschützen Bataillon, now turned into the divisional recce unit, and an army anti-aircraft battalion (Heeres-Flak Abteilung) was attached as a fourth battalion to the Artillerie Regiment. In late 1942 practically every Schützen – or Panzergrenadier, as they had been renamed on 5 July 1942 – Brigade Stab was disbanded or detached.

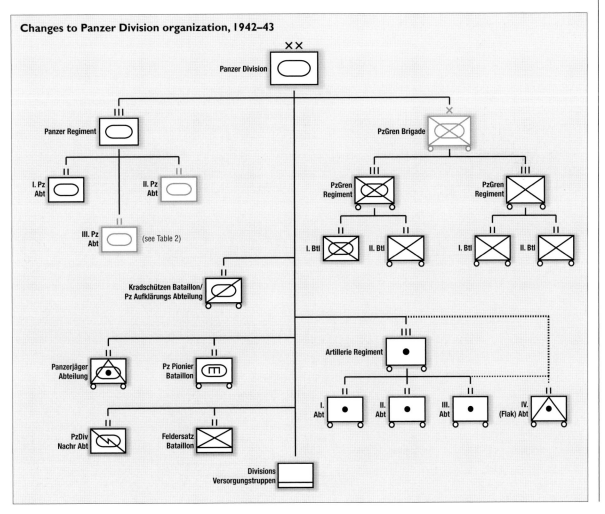

Changes to Panzer Division organization, 1942–43

Panzer Division	Stab Panzer Brig.	Panzer Regiment	Schtz/PzG Brig.St. (SCHWERE IG KOMPANIE)	Schtz. /PzGren Regiment	Kradschützen Btl.	Pz. Aufklärungs Abt., 1941 (1943)
1		1	1 (702)	1, 113	1	4 (1)
2	2	3	2 (703)	2, 304	2	5 (2)
3	5	6	3	3, 394	3	1 (3)
4		35	4	12, 33	34	7 (4)
5		31	5 (704)	13, 14	55	8 (5)
6		11	6	4, 114	6	57 (6)
7		25	7 (705)	6, 7	7	37 (7)
8		10	8	8, 28	8	59 (8)
9		33	9 (701)	10, 11	59	9 (9)
10	4	7	10 (706)	69, 86	10	90 (10)
11		15	11	110, 111	61	231 (11)
12		29	12	5, 25	22	2 (12)
13		4	13	66, 93	43	13 (13)
14		36	14	103, 108	64	40 (14)
16		2	16	64, 79	16	16 (16)
17		39	17	40, 63	17	27 (17)
18	18	18	18	52, 101	18	88 (18)
19		27	19	73, 74	19	19 (19)
20		21	20	59, 112	20	92 (20)
22		204	22	129, 140	24	
23		201 / 23	23	126, 128	23	(23)
24		24	24	21, 26	4	(24)
25		9		146, 147	87	(25)
26		26		9, 67	26	(26)
27		[127]		140		(127)

Table 1: 1–27. Panzer Divisions, 1941–1943: organization and unit numbering (15 and 21. Panzer Divisions exclude

The original caption reads: 'The German Panzer knows no obstacle.' A leichte Panzer Kompanie is negotiating a stream during its advance across central Russia in October 1941. The difficult terrain encountered in the Soviet Union provided plenty of such obstacles.

Artillerie/Panzer Artillerie Regiment	Panzerjäger Abt.	FLA KOMPANIE (H-Flak Abt.)	Pz. Pionier Btl.	PzDiv Nachr. Abt.	Feldersatz Btl/ Versorgungstr.
73	37	2./59, 4./55 (299)	37	37	81
74	38	2./47 (273)	38	38	82
75	543	6./59 (314)	39	39	83
103	49	5./66 (290)	79	79	84
116	53	2./55 (288)	89	77	85
76	41	3./46 (298)	57	82	57
78	42	3./59 (296)	58	83	58
80	43	4./48 (286)	59	84	59
102	50	3./47 (287)	86	85	60
90	90	3./55	49	90	90
119	61	1./608 (277)	209	341 / 89	61
2	2	4./52 (303)	32	2	2
13	13	4./66 (271)	4	13	13
4	4	2./608 (276)	13	4	4
16	16	6./66 (274)	16	16	16
27	27	1./66 (297)	27	27	27
88	88	631 (292)	98	88	88
19	19	(272)	19	19	19
92	92	[10./92]	92	92	92
140	140	632 (289)	50	140	140
128	128	633 (278)	51	128	128
89	40	634 (283)	40	86	40
91	87	(279)	87	87	87
93	93	(304)	93	93	93
127	127		127	127	127

Following the crisis of Stalingrad and the appointment of Guderian as Generalinspekteur der Panzertruppen (inspector general of armoured troops) in January 1943, a new reorganization took place. The Kradschützen Bataillon was renamed Panzer Aufklärungs Abteilung and, most importantly, Panzer Regiments reverted to the standard two-battalion organization. However, since one Panzer Abteilung from every regiment was to be re-equipped with Panther tanks, most Panzer Regiments were left with a single battalion for many months to come.

Lacking overall establishments, and given that several war establishment charts (Kriegsstärke Nachweisungen, or KStN) were lost, it is extremely difficult to assess the Panzer Divisions' overall strength. By June 1941 it stood at c. 13,300 for the standard two-Panzer Abteilung division, though it eventually rose to 15,600 including the third Panzer Abteilung, the Heeres-Flak Abteilung and the full-strength Feld Ersatz Bataillon. AFVs apart, overall weaponry increased dramatically between 1941 and 1943. Additionally, since 1942 foreign personnel, mostly of Soviet origin, were added as Hiwi, or Hilfswillige (auxiliary volunteers).

The Panzer Regiment

The basic organization of the Panzer Regiment did not undergo major changes between 1940 and 1943. Only with the revised KStN of 1 November 1941 were the regimental Nachrichten (communication) and leichter Panzer Zug (light tank platoon) brought under the direct control of the regimental Stab, though without forming a Stabskompanie (HQ coy). Changes mainly affected the number and organization of the Panzer Abteilung in a regiment; in 1941 the basic organization of a Panzer Abteilung was similar to that of the 1 September 1939 establishment, and only the leichte Kolonne (light column) was detached to the divisional supply battalion. The 1 February 1941 KStN of both the leichte (light) and mittlere (medium) Panzer Kompanie were likewise similar to those of 1 September 1939, and the main change introduced by the 1 November 1941 revised KStN was the addition to the Pionier Zug of the Abteilung Stabskompanie (the engineer platoon of the battalion HQ coy) of three PzKpfw IIs. The basic organization of a 1941 Panzer Regiment thus included a regimental Stab with one PzKpfw III, two PzBefh and five PzKpfw II; the Abteilung Stab had the same allowance, eventually increasing to eight PzKpfw II. Each one of the two leichte Panzer Kompanien had 17 PzKpfw III and five PzKpfw II, while the mittlere Panzer Kompanie had 14 PzKpfw IV and five PzKpfw II for a total of 45 PzKpfw II, 71 PzKpfw III and 28 PzKpfw IV, plus six PzBefh in a basic Panzer Regiment (the Staffel, with spare tanks, excluded).

In June 1941 the Panzer Regiments of only eight Panzer Divisions (1, 2, 5, 9, 11, 13, 14 and 16) followed this basic organization, while Panzer Regiment 7 and 35 had three leichte and a mittlere Panzer Kompanie to each Panzer Abteilung. Their establishment was 55 PzKpfw II, 105 PzKpfw III, 28 PzKpfw IV and six PzBefh. Eight other Panzer Regiments (6, 10, 11, 18, 21, 27, 29 and 39) had three Panzer Abteilungen, each with two leichte and a mittlere Panzer Kompanie. Their establishment included 65 PzKpfw II, 106 PzKpfw III, 42 PzKpfw IV and eight PzBefh, while Panzer Regiment 25 of 7. Panzer Division had three Panzer Abteilungen each with three leichte and a mittlere Panzer Kompanie (its establishment was 80 PzKpfw II, 157 PzKpfw III, 42 PzKpfw IV and eight PzBefh) (see Table 2). Obviously, the actual AFV allowance was quite different since five of the three Abteilung Panzer regiments were equipped with the old Czech PzKpfw 38 (t) tanks (Panzer Regiments 10, 11, 21, 25 and 27), while Panzer Regiment 25 was equipped with the older PzKpfw 35 (t); both were used to replace the PzKpfw III and II. All the Panzer Regiments had a single Panzer Werkstatt Kompanie (tank maintenance company) with the exception of those parts of the 6, 7, 8 and 17. Panzer Divisions that also had a

---

Table 2: Panzer Regiment composition in the Panzer Divisions on the Eastern Front, June 1941 to June 1943

(Italic type indicates unit equipped with Czech or captured French tanks)

1941	1942	1943
1. PzDiv	**II./PzRgt 1** (3 Kp), renamed 1943 –	I. / PzRgt 1 [on Panther]
I–II./PzRgt 1 (3 Kp)	I./PzRgt 1 became PzAbt 116 (16. PzGrenDiv)	**II./PzRgt 1** (4 Kp) [new]
2. PzDiv	**II./PzRgt 3** (3 Kp)	**II./PzRgt 3** (4 Kp)
I–II./PzRgt 3 (3 Kp)	I./PzRgt 3 became III./PzRgt 33 (9. PzDiv)	[new I./PzRgt 3 on Panther]
3. PzDiv	**I–III./PzRgt 6** (3 Kp)	**II./PzRgt 6** (4 Kp) [III disbanded]
I–III./PzRgt 6 (3 Kp)		[I./PzRgt 6 on Panther]
4. PzDiv	**I./PzRgt 35** (4 Kp)	**I./PzRgt 35** (4 Kp)
I–II. /PzRgt 35 (4 Kp)	II./PzRgt 35 became III./PzRgt 15 (11. PzDiv)	

 (Table continues on page 15)

5. PzDiv	I–II./PzRgt 31 (4 Kp)	II./PzRgt 31 (4 Kp)
I–II./PzRgt 31 (3 Kp)		[I./PzRgt 31 on Panther]
6. PzDiv	I–II./PzRgt 11 (4 Kp)	II./PzRgt 11 (4 Kp)
I–III. /PzRgt 11 (3 Kp) *	III./PzRgt 11 (PzAbt 65) disbanded	[I./PzRgt 11 on Panther]
7. PzDiv	I–II./PzRgt 25 (4 Kp)	I–II./PzRgt 25 (3 Kp)
I–III./PzRgt 25 (4 Kp)	III./PzRgt 25 disbanded	
8. PzDiv	I. /PzRgt 10 (3 Kp) [III. detached Sept.]	I./PzRgt 10 (4 Kp)
I–III. /PzRgt 10 (3 Kp)	II./PzRgt 10 became III./PzRgt 2 (16. PzDiv)	
9. PzDiv	I–III./PzRgt 33 (3 Kp)	I./PzRgt 33 (4 Kp) [III detached]
I–II./PzRgt 33 (3 Kp)	(III. from I./PzRgt 3)	[II./PzRgt 33 on Panther]
10. PzDiv	I./PzRgt 7 became III./PzRgt 36 (14. PzDiv)	(To Tunisia, disbanded in May)
I–II./PzRgt 7 (4 Kp)		
11. PzDiv	I–III./PzRgt 15 (3 Kp)	II–III./PzRgt 15 (3 Kp)
I–II./PzRgt 15 (3 Kp)	(III. from II./PzRgt 35)	[I./PzRgt 15 on Panther]
12. PzDiv	I–II./PzRgt 29 (3 Kp)	II./PzRgt 29 (4 Kp)
I–III. /PzRgt 29 (3 Kp)	III./PzRgt 29 became III./PzRgt 4 (13. PzDiv)	[I./PzRgt 29 on Panther]
13. PzDiv	I–III./PzRgt 4 (3 Kp)	I–II./PzRgt 4 (3 Kp)
I–II./PzRgt 4 (3 Kp)	(III. from III./PzRgt 29)	[III./PzRgt 4 on Panther]
14. PzDiv	I–III./PzRgt 36 (3 Kp)	[New I–II./PzRgt 36 forming in Germany]
I–II./PzRgt 36 (3 Kp)	(III. from III./PzRgt 7)	
16. PzDiv	I–III./PzRgt 2 (3 Kp)	[New I–II./PzRgt 2 forming in Germany]
I–II./PzRgt 2 (3 Kp)	(III. from II./PzRgt 10)	
17. PzDiv	II./PzRgt 39 (3 Kp) [III. detached 1941]	II./PzRgt 39 (4 Kp)
I–III./PzRgt 39 (3 Kp) +	I./PzRgt 39 became PzAbt 129 (29. PGD)	
18. PzDiv	I. became PzAbt 160 (60. PGD)	II./PzRgt 18 (3 Kp), became
I–III./PzRgt 18 (3 Kp)	III. became PzAbt 103 (3. PGD)	PzAbt 18 (4 Kp)
19. PzDiv	I. /PzRgt 27 (4 Kp); [III. disbanded 1941]	I–II./PzRgt 27 (4-3 Kp)
I–III. /PzRgt 27 (3 Kp) #	(I. disb. 1942), (II. became I./PzRgt 27)	(II./PzRgt 27 rebuilt)
20. PzDiv	III. /PzRgt 21 (4 Kp), became –	PzAbt 21 (4 Kp) (Regiment Stab
I–III. /PzRgt 21 (3 Kp)	(I-II./PzRgt 21 disbanded)	disbanded in April)
22. PzDiv	I–III. /PzRgt 204 (3 Kp) [re-equipped]	(PzRgt 204 is disbanded)
III. /PzRgt 204 (3 Kp)	(new III later to 27. PzDiv, became PzAbt 127)	
23. PzDiv	I–III./PzRgt 201 (3 Kp)	I./PzRgt 201 (4 Kp) **
I–II./PzRgt 201 (3 Kp)	(new III disbanded 1943)	[II./PzRgt 201 on Panther]
24. PzDiv	I–III./PzRgt 24 (3 Kp)	[New I–II./PzRgt 24 forming in Germany]
I–III./PzRgt 24 (3 Kp)		
	27. PzDiv	[disbanded]
	PzAbt 127 (from III./PzRgt 204)	

Notes

* III./Panzer Regiment 11 retained the name of Panzer Abteilung 65.

+ III./Panzer Regiment 39 was formed from I./Panzer Lehr Regiment (equipped with Tauchpanzer); it was attached to the division on 1 June and detached on 16 August.

III./Panzer Regiment 27 was disbanded on 10 August 1941.

** Redesignated Panzer Regiment 23 on 16 August 1943.

Basic organization of a Panzer Regiment, 1 February and 1 November 1941 establishment

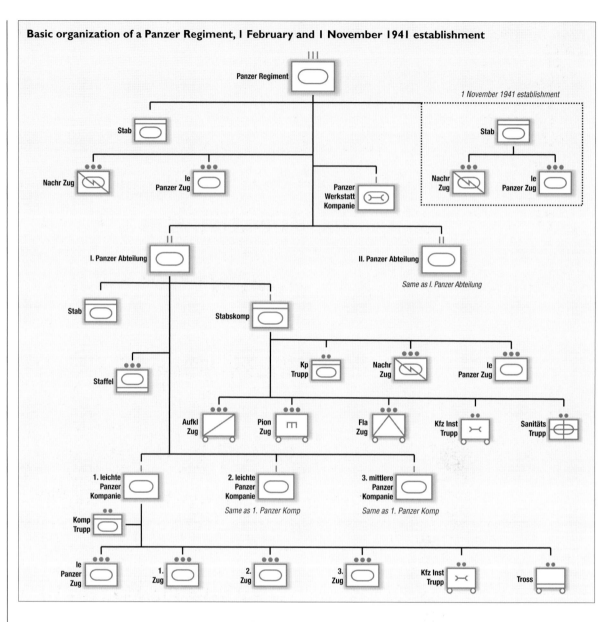

Panzer Werkstatt platoon attached to their third Abteilung, while the Panzer Regiments of 12, 18 and 19. Panzer Divisions had three Panzer Werkstatt Zug.

A comparison between established tank strengths of May 1940 and June 1941 shows that the overall reduction in strength was not only smaller than often reported, but that it mainly affected light tanks. 1. Panzer Division shrank from 118 to 45 light tanks (PzKpfw I and II), 101 to 71 PzKpfw III and 42 to 28 PzKpfw IV, but 2. Panzer Division only saw a reduction from 145 to 45 light tanks and 32 to 28 PzKpfw IV, while actually increasing the number of PzKpfw III (from 60 to 71). (10. Panzer Division increased even further, from 60 to 105.) 3. Panzer Division saw only a dramatic reduction in the number of its light tanks, from 234 (64 of which were PzKpfw I) to 65, while it actually increased its allowance of PzKpfw III (from 16 to 106) and PzKpfw IV (from 24 to 42 – see Table 3 on page 18).

Reorganization in 1942 brought several changes (see Table 2 on page 14). Five Panzer Abteilungen were disbanded and one was detached, three Panzer Divisions transferred four Panzer Abteilungen to the Panzergrenadier Divisions

Panzer Regiment tank establishment, 1 February and 1 November 1941 (light grey)

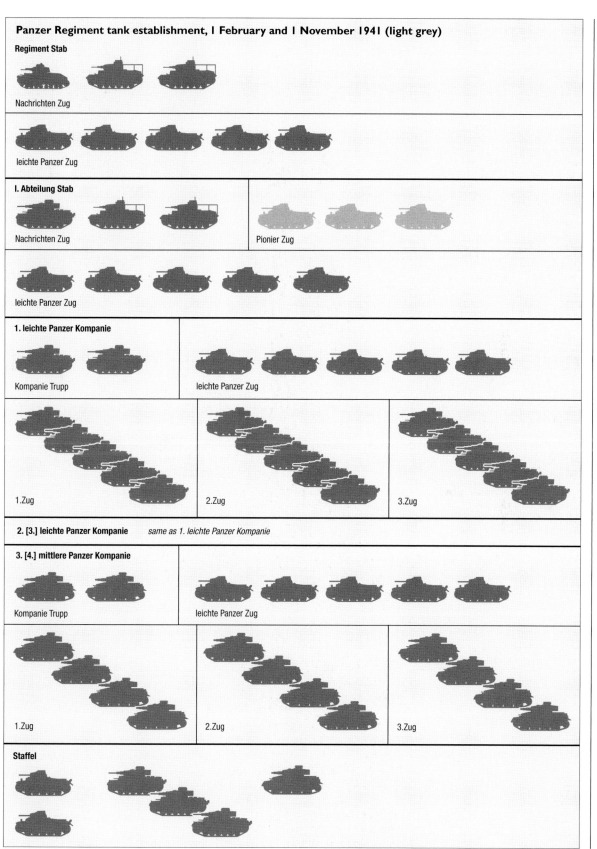

Regiment Stab

Nachrichten Zug

leichte Panzer Zug

I. Abteilung Stab

Nachrichten Zug

Pionier Zug

leichte Panzer Zug

1. leichte Panzer Kompanie

Kompanie Trupp

leichte Panzer Zug

1.Zug

2.Zug

3.Zug

2. [3.] leichte Panzer Kompanie   *same as 1. leichte Panzer Kompanie*

3. [4.] mittlere Panzer Kompanie

Kompanie Trupp

leichte Panzer Zug

1.Zug

2.Zug

3.Zug

Staffel

Table 3: Panzer Division tank strength (Panzer Regiment only), 22 June to August/September 1941

Division	Date		Pz II		Pz III / 35t / 38t		Pz IV		PzBefh
1. PzDiv	22 June =	(45)	43 Pz II	(71)	71 Pz III	(28)	20 Pz IV	(6)	11 PzBefh
	10 Sept. =				43 Pz III [15 w/o]		10 Pz IV [7 w/o]		
3. PzDiv	22 June =	(65)	58 Pz II	(106)	29 + 81 Pz III	(42)	32 Pz IV	(8)	15 PzBefh
	4 Sept. =				6 Pz III [35 w/o]		5 Pz IV [12 w/o]		
4. PzDiv	22 June =	(55)	44 Pz II	(105)	31 + 74 Pz III	(28)	20 Pz IV	(6)	8 PzBefh
	9 Sept. =				24 Pz III [22 w/o]		11 Pz IV [4 w/o]		
6. PzDiv	22 June =	(65)	47 Pz II	(106)	155 Pz 35 t	(42)	30 Pz IV	(8)	13 PzBefh
	9 Sept. =			[+2]	102 Pz 35 t [47 w/o]		21 Pz IV [6 w/o]		
7. PzDiv	22 June =	(80)	53 Pz II	(157)	167 Pz 38 t	(42)	30 Pz IV	(8)	15 PzBefh
	6 Sept. =			[+21]	62 Pz 38 t [59 w/o]		14 Pz IV [9 w/o]		
8. PzDiv	22 June =	(65)	49 Pz II	(106)	118 Pz 38 t	(42)	30 Pz IV	(8)	15 PzBefh
	10 Sept. =				78 Pz 38 t [20 w/o]		17 Pz IV [6 w/o]		
9. PzDiv	22 June =	(45)	8 Pz I / 32 Pz II	(71)	11 + 60 Pz III	(28)	20 Pz IV	(6)	12 PzBefh
	5 Sept. =			[+2]	31 Pz III [14 w/o]	[+1]	6 Pz IV [3 w/o]		
10. PzDiv	22 June =	(55)	45 Pz II	(105)	105 Pz III	(28)	20 Pz IV	(6)	12 PzBefh
	4 Sept. =				75 Pz III [19 w/o]		18 Pz IV [1 w/o]		
11. PzDiv	22 June =	(45)	44 Pz II	(71)	24 + 47 Pz III	(28)	20 Pz IV	(6)	8 PzBefh
	5 Sept. =			[+7]	21 Pz III [24 w/o]	[+2]	4 Pz IV [4 w/o]		
12. PzDiv	22 June =	(65)	40 Pz I /33 Pz II	(106)	109 Pz 38 t	(42)	30 Pz IV	(8)	8 BehPz
	26 Aug. =			[+7]	42 Pz 38 t [47 w/o]		14 Pz IV [8 w/o]		
13. PzDiv	22 June =	(45)	45 Pz II	(71)	27 + 44 Pz III	(28)	20 Pz IV	(6)	13 PzBefh
	28 Aug. =			[+2]	37 Pz III [10 w/o]	[+1]	9 Pz IV [10 w/o]		
14. PzDiv	22 June =	(45)	45 Pz II	(71)	15 + 56 Pz III	(28)	20 Pz IV	(6)	11 PzBefh
	6 Sept. =			[+4]	49 Pz III [17 w/o]	[+1]	15 Pz IV [6 w/o]		
16. PzDiv	22 June =	(45)	45 Pz II	(71)	23 + 48 Pz III	(28)	20 Pz IV	(6)	10 PzBefh
	22 Aug. =				26 Pz III [16 w/o]		9 Pz IV [10 w/o]		
17. PzDiv	22 June =	(65)	44 Pz I /12 Pz II	(106)	106 Pz III	(42)	30 Pz IV	(8)	10 PzBefh
	10 Sept. =				20 Pz III [39 w/o]		4 Pz IV [11 w/o]		
18. PzDiv	22 June =	(65)	6 Pz I / 50 Pz II	(106)	99 + 15 Pz III	(42)	36 Pz IV	(8)	12 PzBefh
	9 Sept. =			[+20]	30 Pz III [21 w/o]	[+5]	16 Pz IV [10 w/o]		
19. PzDiv	22 June =	(65)	42 Pz I /35 Pz II	(106)	110 Pz 38 t	(42)	30 Pz IV	(8)	11 PzBefh
	25 Aug. =				57 Pz 38 t [21 w/o]		9 Pz IV [10 w/o]		
20. PzDiv	22 June =	(65)	44 Pz I /31 Pz II	(106)	121 Pz 38 t	(42)	31 Pz IV	(8)	2 PzBefh
	25 Aug. =			[+14]	52 Pz 38 t [37 w/o]		11 Pz IV [8 w/o]		
2. PzDiv	September	(55)	63 Pz II	(105)	105 Pz III	(28)	20 Pz IV	(6)	6 PzBefh
5. PzDiv	September	(55)	55 Pz II	(105)	105 Pz III	(28)	20 Pz IV	(6)	6 PzBefh

The figures read as follows: in brackets and bold is the established strength; this is followed by actual tank strength. For the PzKpfw III the first figure (if shown) indicates 37mm gun-armed tanks, the second (sometimes the only) figure indicates 50mm gun-armed tanks. The line below, showing tank strength on the given date (PzKpfw III and IV only), includes replacements and the total number of write-offs – both of which are in square brackets.

and five other Panzer Divisions handed one Panzer Abteilung over to sister units. Since a new, third Panzer Abteilung was created in the newly raised or re-equipped 22, 23 and 24. Panzer Divisions, the overall situation by mid-1942 (10. Panzer Division excluded) was as follows: seven Panzer Divisions had a single Panzer Abteilung, four with two leichte and a mittlere Panzer Kompanien (1, 2, 17 and 18. Panzer Divisions) and three others with three leichte and a mittlere Panzer Kompanien (4, 19 and 20. Panzer Divisions); five had two Panzer Abteilungen, two with three (8 and 12. Panzer Divisions, the former until September) and three with four Panzer Kompanien (5, 6 and 7. Panzer Divisions). Also, nine Panzer Divisions had the three-Panzer-Abteilung Panzer Regiment, each with two leichte and one mittlere Panzer Kompanien. Of these only 3. Panzer Division retained its original

A column of dismounted Schützen crosses a frozen Russian river in November 1941. German soldiers often used white sheets for camouflage; unfortunately, they offered almost no protection from the cold.

organization, while five (9, 11, 13, 14 and 16. Panzer Divisions) had the third Panzer Abteilung attached from other divisions, and three others (22, 23 and 24. Panzer Divisions) were newly raised. Now all the Panzer Regiments – except III. Panzer Regiment 21, which had only a Zug – had a Panzer Werkstatt Kompanie, while the Staffel disappeared. Established tank strength of the three-battalion Panzer Regiment was 74 PzKpfw II, 106 PzKpfw III, 42 PzKpfw IV and eight PzBefh. The single, three-company battalion Panzer Regiment had 28 PzKpfw II, 36 PzKpfw III, 14 PzKpfw IV and four PzBefh. (18. Panzer Division had fewer, since the regimental Stab was disbanded by mid-June.) Established strength of the four-company, single-battalion Panzer Regiment was 33 PzKpfw II, 53 PzKpfw III, 14 PzKpfw IV and two PzBefh (again, with fewer for 20. Panzer Division, which had no regimental Stab); 8 and 12. Panzer Divisions had 51 PzKpfw II, 71 PzKpfw III, 28 PzKpfw IV and six PzBefh while 5. Panzer Division had 61 PzKpfw II (21 for both 6 and 7. Panzer Divisions), 105 PzKpfw III, 28 PzKpfw IV (20 for the two other divisions) and six PzBefh – see tables 2 and 5 (the latter on page 64).

Although no major changes were introduced in the revised KStN of 1 November 1941, actual tank availability had a significant organizational impact. The lack of PzKpfw II tanks led to the abandonment of the leichte Panzer Zug in the Panzer Kompanie and the equipping of the Pionier Zug of the Panzer Abteilung's Stabskompanie. Rather, any available PzKpfw II tanks were gathered together in the regimental and battalion leichte Panzer Zug, now equipped with seven rather than the customary five tanks. Moreover, new tank

A reconnaissance unit in 1942, probably a lightly armoured Schützen Kompanie. The lead vehicle, an SdKfz 250/10, is sporting some unusual frontal armour.

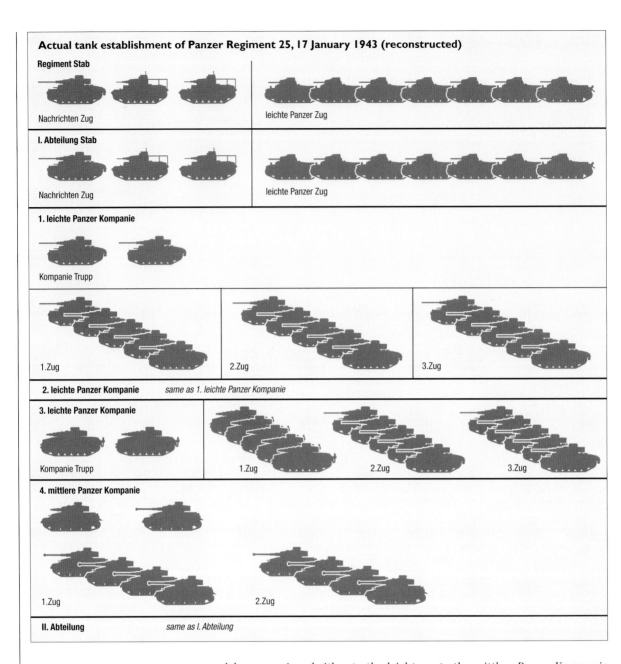

Actual tank establishment of Panzer Regiment 25, 17 January 1943 (reconstructed)

Regiment Stab — Nachrichten Zug / leichte Panzer Zug

I. Abteilung Stab — Nachrichten Zug / leichte Panzer Zug

1. leichte Panzer Kompanie — Kompanie Trupp / 1.Zug / 2.Zug / 3.Zug

2. leichte Panzer Kompanie — *same as 1. leichte Panzer Kompanie*

3. leichte Panzer Kompanie — Kompanie Trupp / 1.Zug / 2.Zug / 3.Zug

4. mittlere Panzer Kompanie — 1.Zug / 2.Zug

II. Abteilung — *same as I. Abteilung*

models were assigned either to the leichte or to the mittlere Panzer Kompanie regardless of their actual purpose; thus the 50mm long-barrelled and 75mm short-barrelled PzKpfw III went to the leichte Panzer Kompanie, while the long-barrelled PzKpfw IV went to the mittlere Panzer Kompanie. Following common practice dating back to 1941, no third Zug was actually formed in the latter due to a shortage of PzKpfw IV tanks.

A new reorganization was started in late January 1943, before Stalingrad fell; new KStN were issued on 25 January for the Panzer Abteilung Stabskompanie and the revised mittlere Panzer Kompanie, intended to replace both the old ones and the leichte Panzer Kompanie. The new Panzer Abteilung included a Stabskompanie with a Nachrichten and an Aufklärungs Zug – the latter replacing the old leichte Panzer Zug, to be equipped with medium tanks. Both the Pionier and Fla (light anti-aircraft) Zug could be formed only by special order, almost like the seven-tank Panzer Flamm Zug

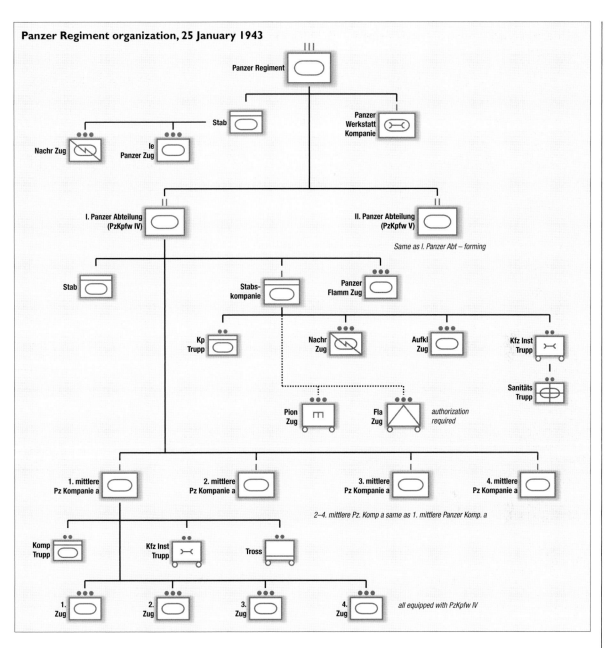

Panzer Regiment organization, 25 January 1943

Panzer Regiment

Nachr Zug

le Panzer Zug

Stab

Panzer Werkstatt Kompanie

I. Panzer Abteilung (PzKpfw IV)

II. Panzer Abteilung (PzKpfw V)

Same as I. Panzer Abt – forming

Stab

Stabs-kompanie

Panzer Flamm Zug

Kp Trupp

Nachr Zug

Aufkl Zug

Kfz Inst Trupp

Sanitäts Trupp

Pion Zug

Fla Zug

authorization required

1. mittlere Pz Kompanie a

2. mittlere Pz Kompanie a

3. mittlere Pz Kompanie a

4. mittlere Pz Kompanie a

2–4. mittlere Pz. Komp a same as 1. mittlere Panzer Komp. a

Komp Trupp

Kfz Inst Trupp

Tross

1. Zug

2. Zug

3. Zug

4. Zug

all equipped with PzKpfw IV

(armoured flame-thrower platoon), which was intended for attachment to the Stabskompanie. Above all, four mittlere Panzer Kompanien, each one with four Zug, became the standard organization for the Abteilung. Each one was to have an establishment of five medium tanks per Zug for a total of 22 tanks in the company and up to 103 of all types in the Abteilung. Following Guderian's appointment as Generalinspekteur der Panzertruppen, a long-term reorganization was begun, addressing which Panzer Regiments were to now have two Panzer Abteilungen, one of which was to be equipped with the new PzKpfw V Panther tank. By June 1943 the reorganization had already been implemented, though not a single Panzer Regiment conformed to its demands. Excluding those divisions either re-forming or still forming, the situation was as follows: ten Panzer Abteilungen were being re-formed (I./PzRgt 1 and 3) or re-equipped in Germany with the Panther, leaving eight divisions (1, 2, 3, 5, 6, 9, 12 and 23. Panzer Divisions) with a single, four-

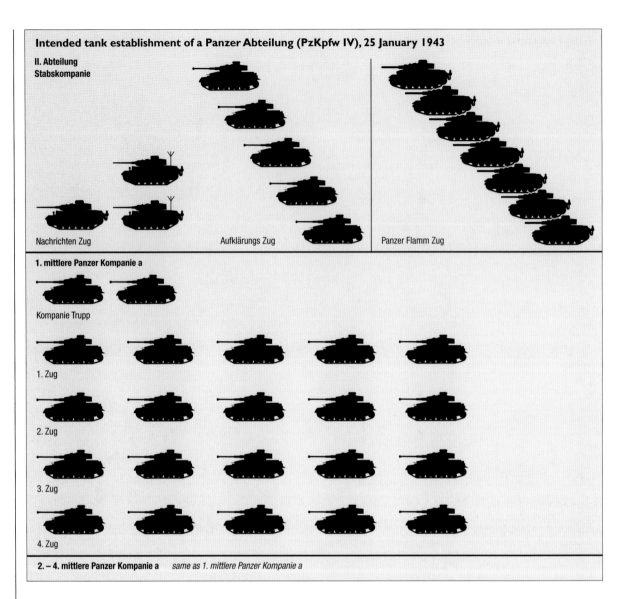

Intended tank establishment of a Panzer Abteilung (PzKpfw IV), 25 January 1943

**II. Abteilung
Stabskompanie**

Nachrichten Zug   Aufklärungs Zug   Panzer Flamm Zug

1. mittlere Panzer Kompanie a

Kompanie Trupp

1. Zug

2. Zug

3. Zug

4. Zug

2. – 4. mittlere Panzer Kompanie a   *same as 1. mittlere Panzer Kompanie a*

A snow-camouflaged Marder II is guided into position, in a photograph taken during the winter of 1942/43. Built on the PzKpfw II chassis from April 1942 onwards, this self-propelled anti-tank gun was armed at first with the captured Soviet 76.2mm PAK 36 gun. The latter was replaced with the German-built 75mm PAK 40 from June 1942. Some 576 examples were produced up to June 1943, with another 75 models converted from the PzKpfw II following until production ceased in March 1944.

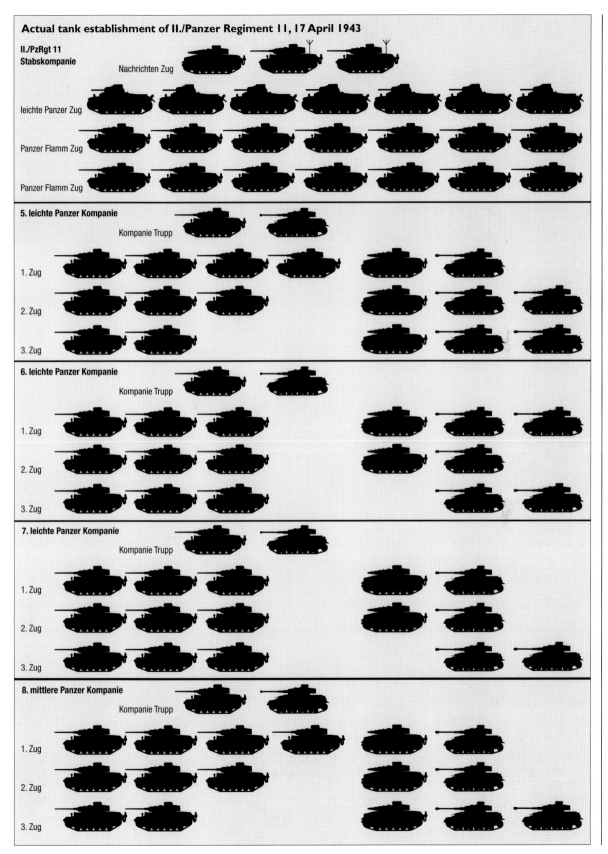

Actual tank establishment of II./Panzer Regiment 11, 17 April 1943

II./PzRgt 11
Stabskompanie

Nachrichten Zug

leichte Panzer Zug

Panzer Flamm Zug

Panzer Flamm Zug

5. leichte Panzer Kompanie

Kompanie Trupp

1. Zug

2. Zug

3. Zug

6. leichte Panzer Kompanie

Kompanie Trupp

1. Zug

2. Zug

3. Zug

7. leichte Panzer Kompanie

Kompanie Trupp

1. Zug

2. Zug

3. Zug

8. mittlere Panzer Kompanie

Kompanie Trupp

1. Zug

2. Zug

3. Zug

company Panzer Abteilung, plus two other divisions with a single Panzer Abteilung and no regimental Stab (18 and 20. Panzer Divisions). Four other divisions had a two-battalions Panzer Regiment (7, 11, 13 and 19. Panzer Divisions) – except for the I./Panzer Regiment 27, which still had three Panzer Kompanien – in most cases with the old organization (see Table 2 on page 14). Only between late August and mid-September did the first Panther Abteilungen join their regiments (I./PzRgt 15 and II./PzRgt 23).

In April 1943 the Panzer Kompanien began to reorganize according to the new mittlere Panzer Kompanie establishment, regardless of their actual designation, though a lack of tanks led to a mixture of different models of PzKpfw III and PzKpfw IV in each Zug, with an average of 18 medium tanks per coy, which still reflected the old organization. Apparently such reorganization was not widespread and was only carried out after new tanks had been delivered to the units.

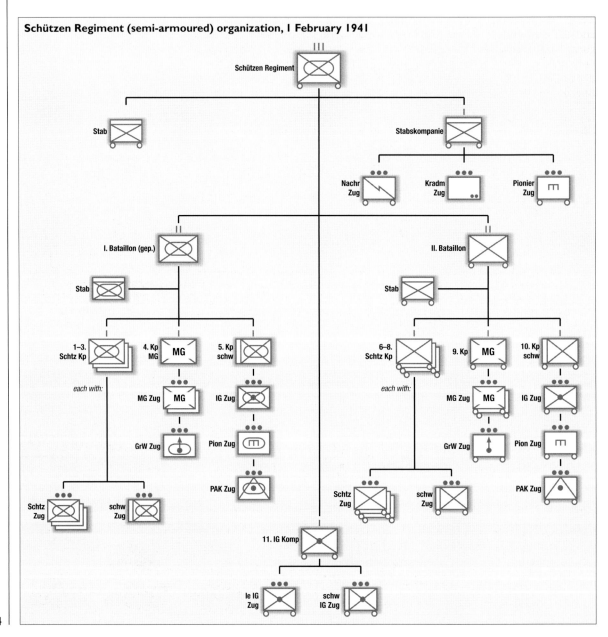

Schützen Regiment (semi-armoured) organization, 1 February 1941

The Schützen/Panzergrenadier Regiment

The basic organization of the 1941 Schützen Brigade included two Schützen Regiments and the Kradschützen Bataillon, later to became the divisional recce unit. The new Schützen Regiment, according to the revised KStN of 1 February 1941, was much stronger than its 1940 counterpart, as was the brigade as a whole. Each regiment included a Stabskompanie with a Nachrichten, a Kradmelde (despatch rider) and a Pionier Zug, plus two Schützen Bataillone each with three Schützen Kompanien (motorized infantry company; each with three infantry and one heavy weapons platoon and a total of 18 light and two heavy MGs, plus three light mortars), a Maschinengewehr Kompanie (MG company with two MGs and a mortar platoon, armed with eight heavy MGs and six heavy mortars) and a schwere Kompanie (heavy weapons company, with an engineer and an anti-tank platoon with three guns). The 11. Infanterie Geschütz Kompanie – companies were numbered in sequence inside the regiment – had two heavy and four light infantry guns. The total strength of the regiment was 2,571, and its weapons allowance included 119 light and 28 heavy MGs, 18 light and 12 heavy mortars, six anti-tank guns, eight light and two heavy infantry guns. Only 13. Panzer Division, whose Schützen Regiment (renamed as such only in May 1941) retained the same organization as the motorized infantry divisions until late 1941, had a different organization. Also six Schützen Brigades (1, 2, 5, 7, 9 and 10. Panzer Divisions) had a self-propelled heavy

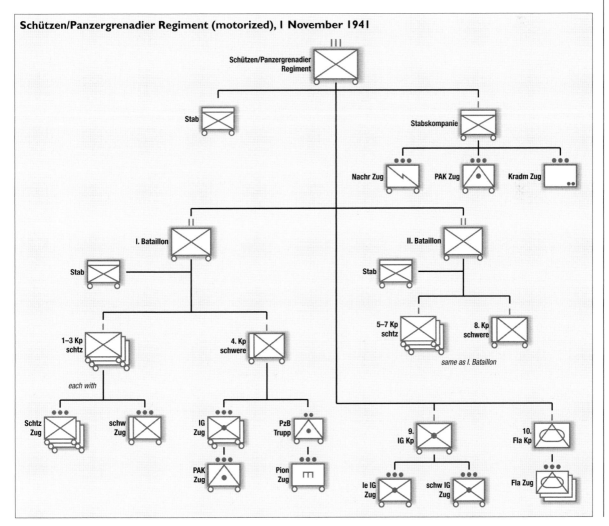

Schützen/Panzergrenadier Regiment (motorized), 1 November 1941

Infanterie Geschütz Kompanie attached. Ideally every Schützen Regiment was to have one gepanzert (armoured) and one motorisiert (motorized) battalion, or at least every brigade was to have one armoured battalion. Lack of equipment led once more to a completely different situation that saw 1. Panzer Division with its full complement of two gepanzerte Schützen Bataillone, while 10. Panzer Division had a single battalion and another 14 divisions had only one single gepanzerte Schützen Kompanie (see Table 4 below).

Experiences in the field and losses suffered during winter 1941/42 led to another reorganization: a three-gun PAK (anti-tank gun) Zug replaced the Pionier Zug in the regimental Stabskompanie, while Maschinengewehr Kompanien were phased out, and the revised KStN of 1 November 1941 brought a completely different weapons allowance. The Schützen – or Panzergrenadier, from 5 July 1942 – Kompanie was now 228 strong and had 18

Table 4: Actual armoured infantry units (gepanzerte Schützen/Panzergrenadier Bataillone) in the Panzer Divisions, 1941–43

	1941	1942	1943 (up to July)
1. PzDiv	I. Btl./Rgt. 1	I. Kp, I. Btl./Rgt. 1 *	
	I. Btl./Rgt. 113	I. Btl./Rgt. 113	I. Btl./Rgt. 113
2. PzDiv		I. Btl./Rgt. 2	
	2. Kp, I. Btl./Rgt. 304	2. Kp, I. Btl./Rgt. 304	I. Btl./Rgt. 304
3. PzDiv	I. Kp, I. Btl./Rgt. 3	I. Btl./Rgt. 3	1-2. Kp, I. Btl./Rgt. 3
		I. Kp, I. Btl./Rgt. 394	
4. PzDiv	I. Kp, I. Btl./Rgt. 12	I. Kp, I. Btl./Rgt. 12	I. Btl./Rgt. 12
5. PzDiv	I. Kp, I. Btl./Rgt. 14	I. Kp, I. Btl./Rgt. 14	I. Kp, I. Btl./Rgt. 14
6. PzDiv	8. Kp, II. Btl./Rgt. 114	II. Btl./Rgt. 114	II. Btl./Rgt. 114
7. PzDiv	I. Kp, I. Btl./Rgt. 6	I. Btl./Rgt. 6	II. Btl./Rgt. 6
8. PzDiv	I. Kp, I. Btl./Rgt. 8	I. Btl./Rgt. 8	I. Kp, I. Btl./Rgt. 8
9. PzDiv	I. Kp, I. Btl./Rgt. 10	I. Btl./Rgt. 10	I. Btl./Rgt. 10
10. PzDiv	II. Btl./Rgt. 69	II. Btl./Rgt. 69	
11. PzDiv	I. Kp, I. Btl./Rgt. 110	1-2. Kp, I. Btl./Rgt. 110	I. Btl./Rgt. 110
12. PzDiv	I. Kp, I. Btl./Rgt. 25	I. Kp, I. Btl./Rgt. 5	
		I. Kp, I. Btl./Rgt. 25	I. Kp, I. Btl./Rgt. 25
13. PzDiv	I. Kp, I. Btl./Rgt. 66	I. Btl./Rgt. 66	I. Btl./Rgt. 66
14. PzDiv		I. Btl./Rgt. 103	I. Btl./Rgt. 103 (forming)
16. PzDiv		(SchtzBtl 16) **	II. Btl./Rgt. 64 (forming)
17. PzDiv	I. Kp, I. Btl./Rgt. 40	1–2. Kp, I. Btl./Rgt. 40	I. Btl./Rgt. 40
18. PzDiv	I. Kp, I. Btl./Rgt. 52	I. Kp, I. Btl./Rgt. 52	I. Kp, I. Btl./Rgt. 52
19. PzDiv			I. Kp, I. Btl./Rgt. 74
20. PzDiv	I. Kp, I. Btl./Rgt. 59		7. Kp, II. Btl./Rgt. 59
22. PzDiv		5-6. Kp., II. Btl./Rgt. 129	
		I. Kp, I. Btl./Rgt. 140	
23. PzDiv		I. Btl./Rgt. 128	I. Btl./Rgt. 128
24. PzDiv		1-2, 4. Kp, I. Btl./Rgt. 26	I. Btl./Rgt. 26 (forming)

Notes

* In April all the available SPW were given to the I. Btl./Rgt. 113 (Bataillon Krieg) that in June had none left.
** Schützen Bataillon 16 formed in April with all the available SPW from Schützen Regiments 64 and 79.

light and four heavy MGs, two heavy mortars and three light Panzerbüchsen (AT rifles). The schwere Kompanie, 169 strong, now included two light infantry guns (only one in 4, 12 17, 19. Panzer Divisions), an engineer and an anti-tank platoon plus an AT rifle section for a total of ten light MGs, four light infantry and three anti-tank guns, plus three AT rifles. All Schützen/Panzergrenadier Regiments also added a four-gun motorized schwere Infanterie Geschütz Kompanie (all but 10. Panzer Division maintained the above-mentioned self-propelled IG Kompanie), and some of them (those part of 3, 9, 11, 13 to 15, 22 to 24. Panzer Divisions) also added a tenth Fla Kompanie (AA company) with 12 self-propelled 20mm anti-aircraft guns, four of which were four-barrelled. Total strength of the Schützen/Panzergrenadier Regiment decreased to 2,223 with an overall weapons allowance of 141 light and 24 heavy MGs, 12 heavy mortars, 9 anti-tank guns, 8 light and 4 heavy infantry guns, 24 AT rifles and 12 anti-aircraft guns. The new Schützen/Panzergrenadier Brigade, without the Kradschützen Bataillon, now had a strength of 4,443 and an armament that included some 300 light and 24 heavy MGs, 24 heavy mortars, 27 anti-tank (37mm and 50mm) and 24 infantry guns. From late 1942, when all the Brigade Stab were either disbanded or detached, the Panzer Divisions were left with two Panzergrenadier Regiments only.

In 1942 the number of gepanzerte Schützen/Panzergrenadier Bataillone increased to a dozen, plus an incomplete one (from 24. Panzer Division), three others with two gepanzerte Schützen/Panzergrenadier Kompanien and eight with a single Kompanie. (The situation varied during the year: in April 1942 all the available Schützenpanzerwagen[1] – or SPW – of 1. Panzer Division went to the I./Schützen Regiment 113, which in June had none left; in April 1942 all the available SPW of 16. Panzer Division were used to form Schützen Bataillon 16 with elements from the Schützen Regiment 64 and 79.) According to the 1 November 1941 establishment, a gepanzerte Schützen/Panzergrenadier Bataillon had a slightly inferior strength to the non-armoured one (913 against 958), but it had more weapons including those mounted on AFVs – 107 light and 12 heavy MGs, 12 anti-tank guns (nine 37mm and three 50mm), six heavy 81mm mortars and four light 75mm infantry guns (non-armoured battalions had 59 light and 12 heavy MGs, six mortars, three anti-tank 50mm and four light infantry guns). The Stab was equipped with four command SdKfz 250/3 half-tracks and two SdKfz 250/2 communications vehicles. Each gepanzerte Schützen/Panzergrenadier

During the German advance through southern Russia in summer 1942, the conditions encountered were not much different from those seen in North Africa. Here soldiers from an unidentified unit of 24. Panzer Division are pushing a leichte Personenkraftwagen (light staff car) along a sand track.

---

1 SPW, subsequently renamed gepanzert Mannschafttransportwagen (MTW), were armoured personnel transport vehicles.

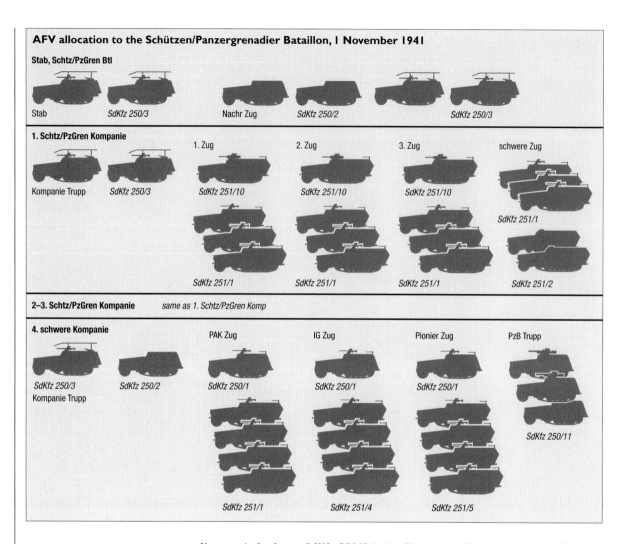

AFV allocation to the Schützen/Panzergrenadier Bataillon, 1 November 1941

Stab, Schtz/PzGren Btl

Stab   SdKfz 250/3   Nachr Zug   SdKfz 250/2   SdKfz 250/3

1. Schtz/PzGren Kompanie

Kompanie Trupp   SdKfz 250/3   1. Zug   2. Zug   3. Zug   schwere Zug

SdKfz 251/10   SdKfz 251/10   SdKfz 251/10   SdKfz 251/1

SdKfz 251/1   SdKfz 251/1   SdKfz 251/1   SdKfz 251/2

2–3. Schtz/PzGren Kompanie   *same as 1. Schtz/PzGren Komp*

4. schwere Kompanie   PAK Zug   IG Zug   Pionier Zug   PzB Trupp

SdKfz 250/3   SdKfz 250/2   SdKfz 250/1   SdKfz 250/1   SdKfz 250/1
Kompanie Trupp

SdKfz 250/11

SdKfz 251/1   SdKfz 251/4   SdKfz 251/5

Kompanie had two SdKfz 250/3 in its Kompanie Trupp (company HQ) plus one 37mm gun-armed SdKfz 251/10 and three APCs SdKfz 251/1 in each one of its three Schützen/Panzergrenadier Zug. The schwere Zug included one SdKfz 251/1 in the Zug Trupp (platoon HQ) and two others in its heavy MG sections, plus two 81mm mortar-equipped SdKfz 251/2 in the mortar section. Total strength was 212 (five officers, 38 NCOs and 169 other ranks), as opposed to the 228 in the non-armoured company (which had 185 other ranks). The gepanzerte schwere Kompanie, which had the same strength as the non-armoured one (169 all ranks), had one SdKfz 250/3 and an SdKfz 250/2 in the Kompanie Trupp, one SdKfz 250/1 plus four SdKfz 251/1 towing three 50mm anti-tanks in the PAK Zug, one SdKfz 250/1 and four SdKfz 251/4 towing four light infantry guns in the IG Zug, one SdKfz 250/1 and four engineer vehicles SdKfz 251/5 in the Pionier Zug and finally three 28mm light anti-tank armed SdKfz 250/11 in the Panzerbüchse Trupp.

The only changes introduced with the revised KStN of 1 April 1943 (1 March and 1 May for the units that formed part of the schwere Kompanie) affected the organization of Stab and Stabskompanie of the gepanzert Panzergrenadier Regiment and the overall organization of the gepanzert Panzergrenadier Bataillon, though by mid-1943 only ten were left, along with four gepanzert Panzergrenadier Regiment Stab (113, 103, 64 plus the reforming 26 – see Table 4 on page 26). Regimental Stabskompanie now included a Nachrichten Zug with four SdKfz 251/3 command vehicles and

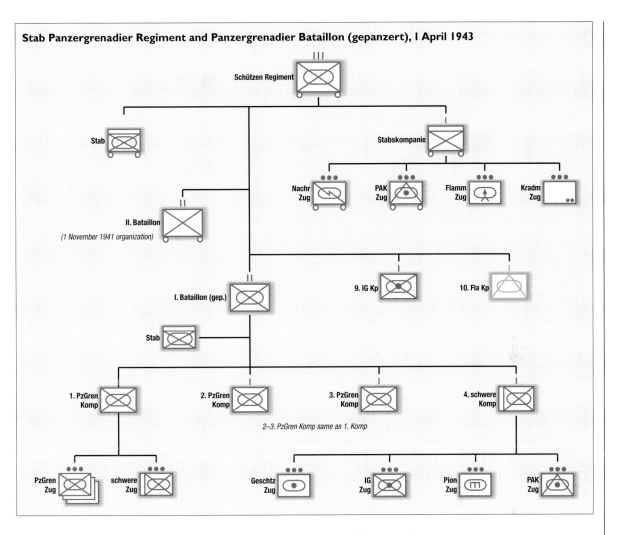

Stab Panzergrenadier Regiment and Panzergrenadier Bataillon (gepanzert), I April 1943

three SdKfz 251/11 communications vehicles, a PAK (anti-tank) Zug with one SdKfz 251/1 and five SdKfz 251/4 towing three 75mm anti-tank guns, a Flammenwerfer (flame-thrower) Zug with six SdKfz 251/16 and the Kradmelde Zug. The gepanzertes Panzergrenadier Bataillon (which included in its Stab two SdKfz 250/3, two SdKfz 251/11, two SdKfz 251/3 and one SdKfz 251/8) had three Panzergrenadier Kompanien each with three Panzergrenadier and one schwere Zug (the only change to the 1 November 1941 KStN was the addition of a 75mm gun-mounted SdKfz 251/9 to the latter), plus a schwere Kompanie with a Geschütz (gun) Zug equipped with one SdKfz 251/1 and six gun-mounted SdKfz 251/9, one Infanterie Geschütz Zug (three SdKfz 251/4 towing two light infantry guns), one Pionier Zug (one SdKfz 250/10 and six engineer SdKfz 251/7 half-tracks) and one PAK Zug with five SdKfz 251/4 towing three 75mm anti-tank guns. (Kompanie Trupp also had one SdKfz 251/3 and one SdKfz 251/11.) Regiments, now some 2,500 strong, also maintained the customary IG Kompanie and, in some cases, the Fla Zug (in the Panzergrenadier Regiment of 1, 3, 9, 11, 13, 14, 16, 23 and 24. Panzer Divisions); only the 2, 5 and 9. Panzer Divisions still had their self-propelled heavy Infanterie Geschütz Kompanie attached.

Reconnaissance units

Until September 1941 every Panzer Division had two recce units: the Kradschützen (motorcycle infantry) Bataillon, part of the Schützen Brigade,

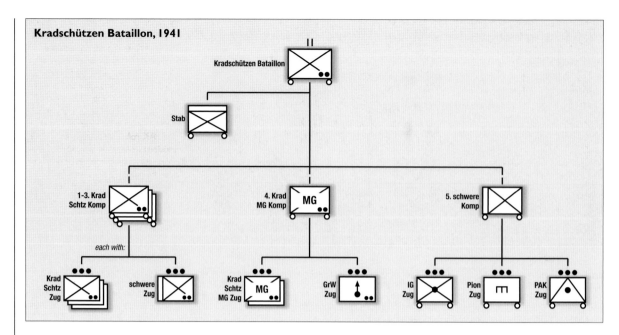

Kradschützen Bataillon, 1941

which used it for its own recce purposes, and the Panzer Aufklärungs Abteilung, the divisional armoured reconnaissance unit. In 1941 the Kradschützen Bataillon, some 1,000 strong, had three Kradschützen Kompanien each with three Kradschützen Zug and a schwere Zug (four officers, 24 NCOs and 150 other ranks; armament included 18 light and two heavy MGs, and three light mortars), one Kradschützen Maschinengewehr Kompanie with two MGs and a Granatenwerfer (mortar) Zug, armed with eight heavy MGs and six heavy mortars, plus a schwere Kompanie with a two-gun Infanterie Geschütz Zug, a Pionier Zug and a three-37mm gun PAK Zug. The Panzer Aufklärungs Abteilung, some 780 strong, had a Panzer Späh (armoured car) Kompanie with two leichte and one schwere Panzer Späh Zug (the former armed with a total of eight SdKfz 221 or 222 and four SdKfz 222 or 223 armoured cars, the latter with three eight-wheeled SdKfz 231 and three 232), one Kradschützen Kompanie

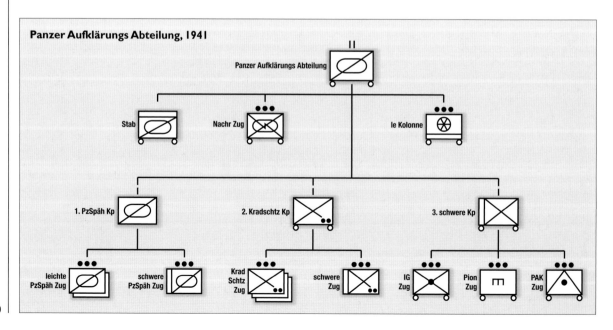

Panzer Aufklärungs Abteilung, 1941

Watched by an 88mm Flak 18 gun, a PzKpfw III Ausf L moves across the Soviet steppe during the summer 1942 offensive (its 50mm KwK 39 L/60 gun has been partly erased from the photograph by the censor). From spring 1942, Heeres Flak Artillerie Abteilung, equipped with the 88mm Flak gun also used in a PAK role, were attached to the divisions to provide additional firepower against the enemy threat from both air and ground.

and a schwere Kompanie with the same organization as those in the Kradschützen Bataillon. Both 7 and 20. Panzer Divisions had two Panzer Späh Kompanien, both equipped with captured French armoured cars.

Experiences during the early stages of *Barbarossa* showed how unsuitable such an organization was; the road-bound Kradschützen Bataillon lacked heavy and armoured vehicles to provide the required punch, while the Panzer Aufklärungs Abteilung, also plagued by widespread lack of armoured cars, lacked infantry strength. A remedy was found in merging the Panzer Aufklärungs Abteilung with the Kradschützen Bataillon, which retained its

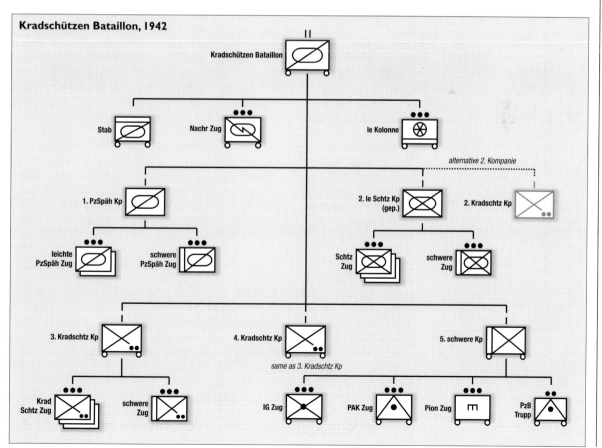

Kradschützen Bataillon, 1942

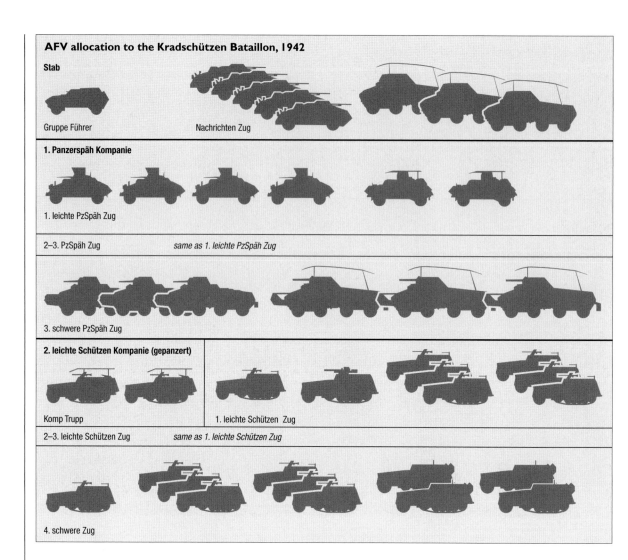

AFV allocation to the Kradschützen Bataillon, 1942

Stab

Gruppe Führer

Nachrichten Zug

1. Panzerspäh Kompanie

1. leichte PzSpäh Zug

2–3. PzSpäh Zug   *same as 1. leichte PzSpäh Zug*

3. schwere PzSpäh Zug

2. leichte Schützen Kompanie (gepanzert)

Komp Trupp

1. leichte Schützen Zug

2–3. leichte Schützen Zug   *same as 1. leichte Schützen Zug*

4. schwere Zug

name and was put under direct control of Panzer Division headquarters. The first to implement the new organization were 2 and 5. Panzer Divisions in September 1941, shortly before their arrival on the Eastern Front. Other divisions reorganized their units in spring 1942, also taking advantage of the new KStN issued on 1 March for a gepanzerte leichte Schützen Kompanie (armoured light infantry company), the first real attempt made to transform the reconnaissance unit into a true combat unit. The 1942 organization of the new Kradschützen Bataillon included a new Stab with a fully armoured Nachrichten Zug (equipped with one SdKfz 247, one SdKfz 260 and four 261 plus three eight-wheeled SdKfz 263 communications armoured cars), one Panzer Späh Kompanie now with a heavy and three light Panzer Späh Zug (for a total of twelve SdKfz 222 and six 223, plus the usual three SdKfz 231 and three 232), one leichte Schützen, two Kradschützen and a schwere Kompanie. Due to the lack of armoured cars, no Panzer Späh Kompanie was present in the Kradschützen Bataillone of 8, 18 and 20. Panzer Divisions.

Owing to a lack of SPWs, only twelve Panzer Divisions (3, 6, 7, 9, 10, 11, 13, 14, 16, 22, 23 and 24) adopted this organization, while the others (1, 2, 4, 5, 8, 12, 17, 18, 19 and 20. Panzer Divisions) replaced the missing leichte Schützen with a Kradschützen Kompanie. The revised KStN (1 November 1941) for the Kradschützen Kompanie led to an increase in strength (five officers, 31 NCOs and 191 other ranks) and weaponry, which now included

Panzer Aufklärungs Abteilung, 1943

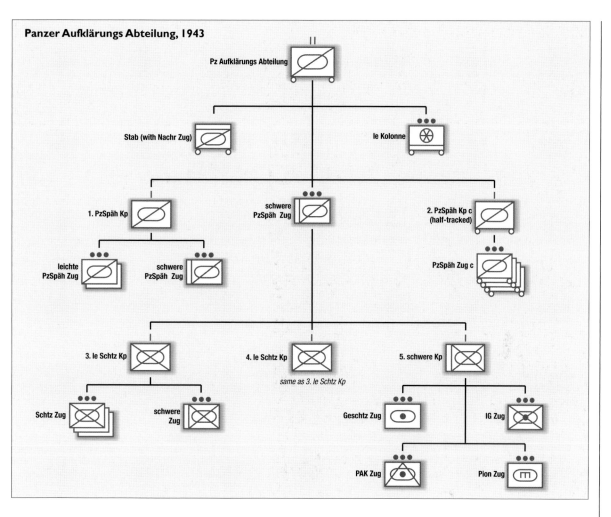

18 light and four heavy MGs, two heavy mortars and three AT rifles. The gepanzerte leichte Schützen Kompanie (five officers, 43 NCOs and 189 other ranks), which featured a similar organization, had 56 light and four heavy MGs, four heavy mortars and three 37mm anti-tank guns including weapons aboard its two SdKfz 250/3 command vehicles, 28 SdKfz 250/1 APCs, three 37mm gun-armed SdKfz 250/10 and four mortar-equipped SdKfz 250/7. The schwere Kompanie added to its organization a Panzerbüchse Trupp and replaced its 37mm anti-tank guns with the newest 50mm models. The total strength of the Kradschützen Bataillon was now about 1,280.

The successful new organization was maintained in 1943 when (following the issue of a new KStN for the Stab on 16 January) Kradschützen Bataillone were renamed Panzer Aufklärungs Abteilungen and renumbered; it was reorganized with a new armoured-car-equipped Geschütz Zug (gun platoon with six 75mm guns), one Panzer Späh Kompanie with armoured cars (unchanged) and a new, half-track-mounted Panzer Späh Kompanie c that had in its four platoons eight SdKfz 250/5 and sixteen 20mm-gun-armed SdKfz 250/9. The Abteilung was also to have two leichte Schützen Kompanien with the same organization and a new schwere Kompanie, now to include a six-gun Geschütz Zug plus the customary Infanterie Geschütz, Pionier and PAK Zug, all to be equipped with half-tracks. By July 1943 only six Panzer Divisions had reorganized their Panzer Aufklärungs Abteilung according to the new establishment, and three of these (14, 16 and 24, other than the 1, 2 and 9. Panzer Divisions) were being rebuilt.

Panzer Artillerie Regiment, 1941–43

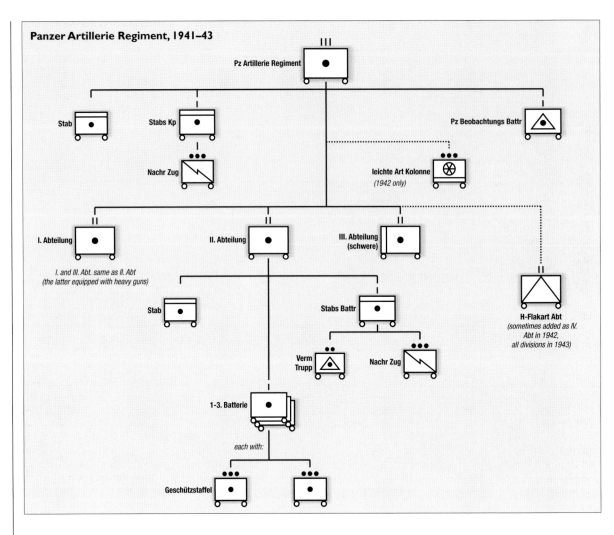

Pz Artillerie Regiment III

Stab

Stabs Kp

Pz Beobachtungs Battr

Nachr Zug

leichte Art Kolonne
(1942 only)

I. Abteilung II

II. Abteilung II

III. Abteilung (schwere) II

I. and III. Abt. same as II. Abt (the latter equipped with heavy guns)

Stab

Stabs Battr

Verm Trupp

Nachr Zug

H-Flakart Abt
(sometimes added as IV. Abt in 1942, all divisions in 1943)

1-3. Batterie

each with:

Geschützstaffel

Heeres Flakartillerie Abteilung, 1942–43

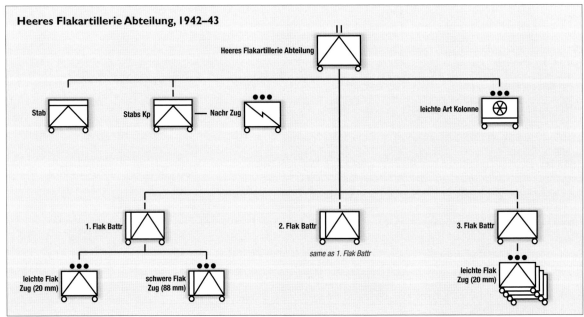

Heeres Flakartillerie Abteilung II

Stab

Stabs Kp — **Nachr Zug**

leichte Art Kolonne

1. Flak Battr

2. Flak Battr

same as 1. Flak Battr

3. Flak Battr

leichte Flak Zug (20 mm)

schwere Flak Zug (88 mm)

leichte Flak Zug (20 mm)

A divisional supply column, part of Kleist's Panzergruppe I, waits for a ferry to carry it across the Dniepr River in October 1941. Supply was a key issue for the Panzer Divisions during *Barbarossa*, given the vaste expanse of territory covered and the poor state of the road network.

Artillery

The Artillerie Regiment, or Panzer Artillerie Regiment since February 1941 (after the issue of the revised KStN on 1 November 1941), now had three Artillerie Abteilungen, each one with three four-gun batteries – either light howitzers 105mm leichte Feldhaubitzen 18 in the leichte Artillerie Abteilung or, in the schwere Artillerie Abteilung, heavy howitzers 150mm schwere Feldhaubitzen 18 and heavy field guns 105mm Kanonen 18 (the latter equipped one battery in the schwere Artillerie Abteilung of 2, 3, 4, 7, 10, 11 and 14. Panzer Divisions). The new KStN issued on 1 February 1941 also created a regimental Stabskompanie that included the fully motorized Nachrichten Zug and the battalion Stabskompanie encompassing the Nachrichten Zug and the Vermessungstrupp (calibration detachment). Both the regimental and the battalion Stabskompanie had one SdKfz 253 armoured observation vehicle, which could be replaced by the SdKfz 250/3. A Panzer Beobachtungs Batterie (armoured spotting battery) was also added; this included a Lichtmess Stellen Staffel (flash ranging detachment), a Vorwarner Trupp (advanced warning section), a Schallmess Stellen Staffel (sound ranging detachment), an Auswerte Staffel (evaluation detachment), a Druckerei and a Wetter Trupp (printing and meteorological sections). Fully motorized, by June 1941 the Beobachtungs Batterien were in the process of getting armoured vehicles, even as several Artillerie Regiments were still forming the new Stabsbatterie. The revised KStN of 1 November 1941 sanctioned the armoured nature of the Beobachtungs Batterie, adding to its establishment thirteen SdKfz 251/12 armoured observation vehicles. A leichte Artillerie Kolonne (light column) was also added, only to disappear early in 1943.

Further changes were dictated by the situation on the field. Although in 1942 most of III. Abteilung of the Panzer Artillerie Regiment had two schwere Feldhaubitzen 18 and one Kanone 18 Batterie (with the exception of 4, 17 and 18. Panzer Divisions), losses actually fell to three guns in the batteries of several divisions (1, 2, 4, 5, 8, 12, 17, 18, 19 and 20. Panzer Divisions). Also, between May and July 1942 several divisions (3, 6, 9, 11, 13, 14, 16, 22, 23 and 24. Panzer Divisions) had a Heeres Flakartillerie Abteilung (army anti-aircraft battalion) attached, eventually becoming the IV. Abteilung of Panzer Artillerie Regiment. This was made up of two Flak Batterien, each with a four 88mm-Flak gun schwere Flak Zug and a three 20mm-gun leichte Flak Zug, plus a third Flak Batterie with twelve 20mm light Flak guns. In spring 1943 the Abteilung, now attached to other divisions as well (the exceptions were 8. Panzer Division,

German war establishment charts: the Kriegsstärke Nachweisungen
Organization, strength, weapons and equipment allowances are normally dictated by war establishment charts or tables of organization and equipment (TO&E). In general these are laid down starting with the main combat unit, namely the division, to every subunit. However, the German Army issued its own war establishment charts, or Kriegsstärke Nachweisung (KStN), based at the lowest level (companies and platoons). This sometimes led to two divisions of the same kind having different organizations and strengths, in spite of the fact they were fighting alongside one another. Only in September 1943 did the Panzer Divisions get a comprehensive and common establishment, though still applying the KStN. Such an elaborate system actually enabled the Germans to reorganize their units according to both their needs and to available manpower, weapons and equipment, right down to the lowest level. Occasionally, single units within the divisions were reorganized, or others maintained their current organization when other units underwent reorganization. Regularly updated, the KStN were put into effect during rest periods or when the unit was pulled out from the front to rest and refit – often months after they had been issued.

which featured it in September, 18. Panzer Division, which no longer had one attached in winter 1942, and 20. Panzer Division, with only a Fla Kompanie), was put under direct control of divisional HQ. The only other change introduced in 1943 was the creation of the first self-propelled Batterie equipped with the 105mm 'Wespe'. By July only two divisions had a full self-propelled Artillerie Abteilung (2 and 4. Panzer Divisions), while nine others only had a single battery (5, 6, 9, 11 and 13. Panzer Divisions; 7. Panzer Division, along with the re-forming 14, 16 and 24. Panzer Divisions, had two batteries).

Anti-tank and engineers

Reorganization of the Panzerjäger Abteilung (anti-tank unit) began as early as July 1940, but in June 1941 only minor improvements had been obtained. The Abteilung was made up of a Stab and a Nachrichten Zug, and included three PAK Kompanien each with two leichte (37mm PAK 35/36) and one mittlere (50mm PAK 38) Zug, with either three or four guns plus six light MGs. The most common establishment included eight 37mm PAK 35/36, four in each Zug, plus three 50mm PAK 38 (in 1, 2, 4, 5, 9 through 14, 16 through 18. Panzer Divisions), the alternate one for all other divisions included six 37mm (three per Zug) and four 50mm guns; only 3. Panzer Division, which had its Panzerjäger Abteilung replaced after handing its own to 5. leichte Division, had twelve 37mm guns. Part of the Abteilung was also a Fla Kompanie made up of two light (four 20mm guns each) and one medium (two 20mm quad) Zug, common to all but three divisions (3, 19 and 20. Panzer Divisions had no Fla Kompanien). The guns were self-propelled, and SdKfz 10/4 and 7/1 half-tracks were used; only the Fla Kompanie in both 17 and 18. Panzer Divisions had four towed four-barrelled 20mm guns.

The inadequacy of the Panzer Divisions' anti-tank defences became clear in 1941, though the lack of weapons did not allow for a proper reorganization. The KStN of 1 November 1941 for the PAK Kompanie simply reversed the ratio in favour of the 50mm guns, now equipping two Zug each with three guns, while one Zug was still armed with four 37mm guns. However, the number of light and medium Zug in the company and the number of guns in each Zug varied according to availability. On 15 February 1942 new KStN were laid down for the PAK Kompanie *selbstfahrlafette* (or sfl – self-propelled), which had three self-propelled anti-tank vehicles ('Marder' II or III) in each of its two Zug. On paper, every Panzerjäger Abteilung was to be equipped with a self-propelled Kompanie plus two motorized ones, but a lack of equipment led to few of the former ever being created and a reduction to two PAK Kompanien. In June 1942 only ten divisions had sfl PAK Kompanien plus a mixture of other companies; 1. Panzer Division had only one sfl and a second motor PAK Kompanie with six 50mm and four 37mm guns, while 2 and 4. Panzer Divisions had two of the latter; 5. Panzer Division's second PAK Kompanie had three 50mm and eight 37mm guns, while both 17 and 18. Panzer Divisions had two of these and 16. Panzer Division added to its sfl PAK Kompanie a second one with nine 50mm guns. The 8, 19 and 20. Panzer Divisions had two sfl Kompanien, with 19 and 20. Panzer Divisions having a third motor PAK Kompanie, the former with nine 50mm guns and the latter with six 50mm and four 37mm guns. Seven other divisions (3, 9 through 12, 23 and 24. Panzer Divisions) had two motor companies

The engine of a PzKpfw IV being overhauled by a maintenance crew. Every Panzer Regiment's Werkstatt Kompanie was deployed together with other divisional supply and service units and, in addition to standard maintenance tasks, repaired all the damaged tanks that could be done within the timeframe available. Extensive damage – that which required more than a week to repair – was handled by depots located back in Germany.

each with nine 50mm guns, while three other divisions (6, 7, 13, 14 and 22) had one of the newly formed (KStN dated 1 June 1942) heavy PAK Kompanien armed with nine 75mm or 76.2mm guns plus another company with nine 50mm guns. 14. Panzer Division had one six-gun 75mm heavy company plus one nine-gun 50mm company, and 22. Panzer Division had two six-gun heavy 76.2mm PAK Kompanien. Again, both 19 and 20. Panzer Division had no Fla Kompanie, and 18. Panzer Division retained its non self-propelled heavy Zug.

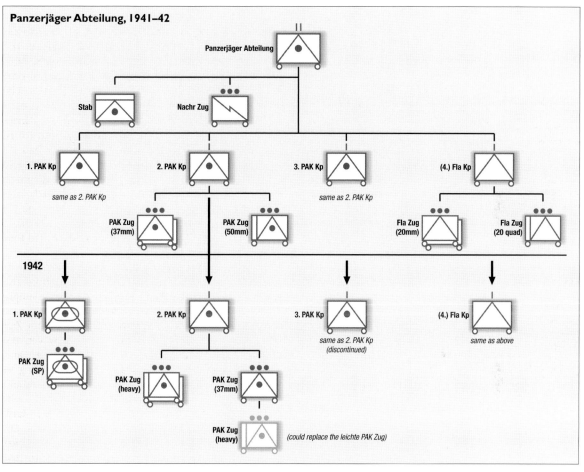

Panzerjäger Abteilung, 1941–42

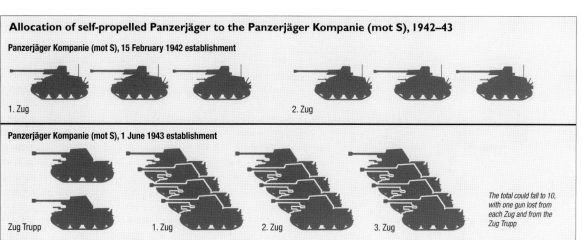

Allocation of self-propelled Panzerjäger to the Panzerjäger Kompanie (mot S), 1942–43

Panzerjäger Kompanie (mot S), 15 February 1942 establishment

1. Zug

2. Zug

Panzerjäger Kompanie (mot S), 1 June 1943 establishment

Zug Trupp

1. Zug

2. Zug

3. Zug

The total could fall to 10, with one gun lost from each Zug and from the Zug Trupp

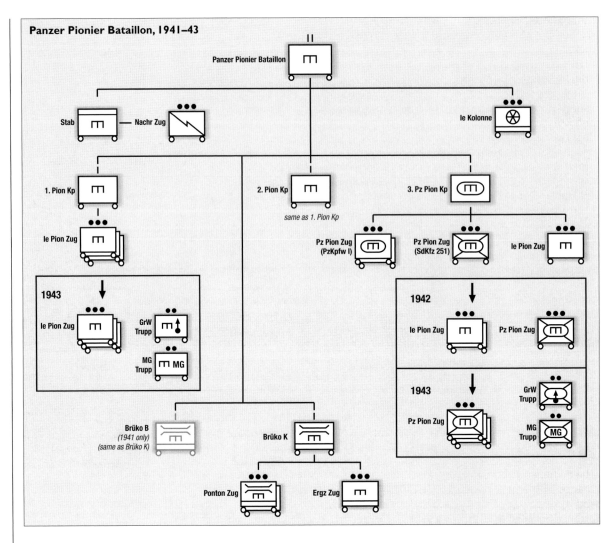

Panzer Pionier Bataillon, 1941–43

Panzer Pionier Bataillon

Stab — Nachr Zug

le Kolonne

1. Pion Kp

le Pion Zug

1943

le Pion Zug

GrW Trupp

MG Trupp — MG

2. Pion Kp

same as 1. Pion Kp

3. Pz Pion Kp

Pz Pion Zug (PzKpfw I)

Pz Pion Zug (SdKfz 251)

le Pion Zug

1942

le Pion Zug

Pz Pion Zug

1943

Pz Pion Zug

GrW Trupp

MG Trupp — MG

Brüko B
(1941 only)
(same as Brüko K)

Brüko K

Ponton Zug

Ergz Zug

In spring 1943 a major reorganization was intended for the Panzerjäger Abteilung, which was to have three sfl PAK Kompanie each with four self-propelled-gun Zug (KStN 1 June 1943), for a total of 14 self-propelled guns. In practice, one self-propelled gun could be absent from each Zug and the Zug Trupp, thus reducing the total to ten guns. In July 1943 this was the organization of the Panzerjäger Abteilung of five divisions (1, 4 with a fourth motor Zug, 11, 13 and 20. Panzer Divisions), while only 2. Panzer Division had a 14-self-propelled-gun Abteilung. Seven other divisions had two 14-gun self-propelled Kompanien (8, 9 and 23; 5, 17, 18 and 19. Panzer Divisions also had a third motor company), while four divisions only had one single-14-gun self-propelled and one 12-gun motor company (3, 6, 7 and 12. Panzer Divisions). Following the attachment to the divisions of the Heeres Flakartillerie Abteilung, the Fla Kompanien were dispensed with.

In 1941, the Panzer Pionier Bataillon was one of the Panzer Divisions' strongest support elements with its 900 men and 200 vehicles. Its first two leichte Pionier Kompanien, mounted on the two-ton Pionier Kampfwagen III lorries, each had three leichte Pionier Zug armed with nine light MGs (18 in 1942) plus combat engineer equipment. In January 1941 the third Panzer Pionier Kompanie was reorganized as a fully armoured coy with a fourth light Zug providing support; the first two Panzer Pionier Zug each had five PzKpfw I Ausf. B (plus one in the Kompanie Trupp) modified to carry a detachable

Ladungsleger (explosive load), while the third Zug had six SdKfz 251 equipped with the Wurfrahmen 40 rocket launcher, a device capable of firing 280mm high-explosive and 320mm incendiary rockets. Bridging equipment was provided by Brückenkolonne B (one per division) and K (not with 17, 18 and 20. Panzer Divisions; 11. Panzer Division had two), each one with two Ponton Zug and an Ergänzung (support) Zug. These could build bridges some 100m long for use by tanks. Shortages, however, led to the withdrawal of Brüko B at the end of 1941, thus leaving the Panzer Divisions with only a single Brüko K (in 1942 it was still absent from 17, 18 and 20. Panzer Divisions).

In winter 1941/42 all the PzKpfw I were lost and, lacking suitable replacements, the first two Panzer Pionier Zug shrank to a single leichte Pionier Zug, thus leaving the third as the only armoured platoon, now equipped with six SdKfz 251/5 and one SdKfz 250/3. A major reorganization took place in 1943 with the revised KStN of 1 March and 1 April; both the leichte and Panzer Pionier Kompanie had a Granatenwerfer and a heavy MG Trupp attached and were now armed with 18 light and two heavy MGs, six flame-throwers, two heavy mortars and three AT rifles; the latter was

Inter-arm (and inter-service) cooperation was seen at every level. Here, an SdKfz 9/1 half-track crane, which had a six-ton lifting capacity, takes a break from its more customary work of hoisting a turret onto a PzKpfw III to help the divisional Schlachterei (butchers) Kompanie.

also equipped with two SdKfz 250/3, 23 SdKfz 251/7 and two SdKfz 251/2. In July 1943 all but six divisions had one Panzer Pionier Kompanie (3, 5, 17, 18, 23 and 25. Panzer Divisions), and 7. Panzer Division had two.

Signals, replacement, supply and divisional services

The divisional signals unit, the Panzer Division Nachrichten Abteilung, did not change its structure in 1941–42, but did suffer from a lack of armoured command and communication vehicles. In 1941 the Nachrichten Abteilung, whose commander was also the Divisions Nachrichten Führer (divisional signals commander), was made up of a Panzer Nachrichten Kompanie and a Panzer Funk Kompanie, both motorized. The first was a communications unit mainly entrusted with laying telephone cable and providing exchanges and as such was primarily active when the division was not on the move (the exception was when one of its three Zug was detached in support of the Schützen Brigade). The company was the wireless and radio communications company that generally speaking had either all or at least two of its three Zug attached both to the Panzer Regiment and divisional Stab. It featured a wide array of armoured command and communications vehicles such as the Panzer Befehls III tank, the SdKfz 251/3 and 251/6 half-tracks, and the SdKfz 260, 261 and eight-wheeled SdKfz 263 armoured cars. Since these were not always available, lorries such as the Kfz 15, 17, 19 and 23 were used as replacements. KStN of 1 November 1941 led to the Panzer Nachrichten Kompanie being renamed the Panzer Fernsprech Kompanie (telephone company) which, like the Panzer Funk Kompanie, was now officially an armoured unit, though mostly on paper. The latter was reorganized with a revised KStN of 1 June 1942, which increased its Zug to four and envisaged a total availability of three PzBefh III and 23 SdKfz 251/3. The Fernsprech Kompanie was reorganized with a KStN dated 1 March 1943; now it had two armoured and two motorized Zug and a total allowance of 14 SdKfz 251/11 and two SdKfz 251/19 telephone exchange and cable-laying half-tracks.

Also in 1941 Panzer Divisions formed their own Feldersatz Bataillon, the field replacement battalion. In spite of its paper organization, which included

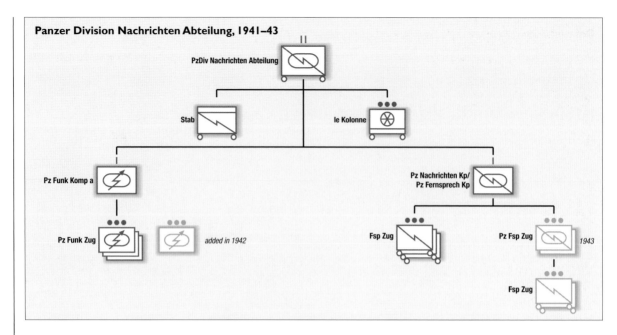

Panzer Division Nachrichten Abteilung, 1941–43

PzDiv Nachrichten Abteilung

Stab

le Kolonne

Pz Funk Komp a

Pz Nachrichten Kp/
Pz Fernsprech Kp

Pz Funk Zug

added in 1942

Fsp Zug

Pz Fsp Zug *1943*

Fsp Zug

a Stab and three companies, the battalion was only about 100 strong and equipped with a selection of weapons and equipment. It would reach full strength only with the arrival at the division of a Marsch Bataillon (march battalion), which would have been split into three, and later four, companies, each one providing replacements to a division's battalion with soldiers trained on the field by experienced personnel (specialists were trained separately). Divisional services, or Rückwärtiger Dienst (rear area services) until June 1941 and from then Versorgungstruppen (supply troops), included administrative (Verwaltungsdienst), field post (Feldpost), military police (Feldgendarmerie), medical (Sanitätsdienst) and supply (Nachschubdienst) units, all under control of the divisional Stab and supervized by the divisional supply officer (also known as I b). Supply units were the most important ones; under the command of the Divisions Nachschub Führer (DiNaFü), later Kommandeur Divisions Nachschubtruppen (KoDiNa), these were reorganized in early 1941. The leichte Infanterie Kolonne of the Schützen Regiment and the leichte Panzer Kolonne of the Panzer Abteilung were used to form two new kleine Kraftwagen Kolonnen (light truck columns) with a 30-ton payload and two or three (according to the number of Panzer Abteilungen) grosse Kraftwagen Kolonnen (heavy truck columns) with a 60-ton payload; adding the former to the seven kleine Kraftwagen Kolonnen already available, each division was to have nine of these plus three heavy columns and three other grosse Kraftwagen Kolonnen für Betriebsstoff (heavy truck fuel columns, with a capacity of 50 cubic metres).

Three essential services in a single image: a dispatch rider, probably from the divisional HQ Kradmelde Zug, asks for information from two Feldgendarmen from the divisional Feldgendarmerie Trupp at a crossroads in front of a Feldlazarett (field hospital), where a Sanitätskraftwagen (ambulance) from the Krankenkraftwagen Zug stands waiting.

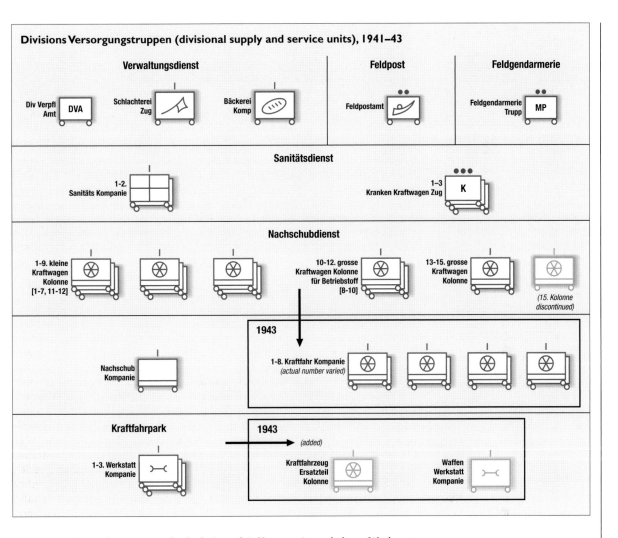

Divisions Versorgungstruppen (divisional supply and service units), 1941–43

Verwaltungsdienst

Div Verpfl Amt — DVA
Schlachterei Zug
Bäckerei Komp

Feldpost

Feldpostamt

Feldgendarmerie

Feldgendarmerie Trupp — MP

Sanitätsdienst

1–2. Sanitäts Kompanie
1–3 Kranken Kraftwagen Zug — K

Nachschubdienst

1–9. kleine Kraftwagen Kolonne [1–7, 11–12]
10–12. grosse Kraftwagen Kolonne für Betriebstoff [8–10]
13–15. grosse Kraftwagen Kolonne
(15. Kolonne discontinued)

1943

Nachschub Kompanie
1–8. Kraftfahr Kompanie (actual number varied)

Kraftfahrpark

1–3. Werkstatt Kompanie

1943

(added)

Kraftfahrzeug Ersatzteil Kolonne
Waffen Werkstatt Kompanie

Also at its disposal were a Nachschub (supply) Kompanie and three Werkstatt (workshop) Kompanien, part of the divisional Kraftfahrpark (vehicles' park). Unsuitability of roads and long distances soon led to heavy attrition which, added to the effects of winter, heavily reduced availability of supply vehicles and led to the use of sledges. In 1942 columns were reshuffled to keep the divisions in southern Russia up to strength, but late in the year a major reorganization took place.

From December, kleine and grosse Kraftwagen Kolonnen were grouped together to form Kraftfahr Kompanien (supply vehicle companies); these were heavier, with either a 90- or 120-ton payload and 33 or 44 trucks (the kleine had 11 and the grosse Kraftwagen Kolonne had 21), but actual numbers shrank to a maximum of eight per division depending on availability of vehicles. In July 1943, most Panzer Divisions had only five of them. Since late 1942 a 60-ton Kraftfahrzeug Ersatzteil Kolonne (vehicles spare parts column) and a Waffen Werkstatt Kompanie (weapons maintenance company) were also added to divisional Kraftfahrpark. No changes took place in the organization of other services; medical units included two motorized Sanitäts Kompanien (medical companies) and three Krankekraftwagen Zug (ambulance platoons), administrative units included the Bäckerei (baker) Kompanie, the Schlachterei (butcher) Kompanie and the Divisions Verpflegungsamt (divisional rations detachment). Both the Feldgendarmerie Trupp (military police platoon) and the Feldpostamt (field post office) were at the direct disposal of divisional HQ.

Tactics

Although the basic tactical principles of German armoured warfare did not change much during the first two years of war on the Eastern Front, the way these were put into practice by the Panzer Divisions varied to a greater extent owing to several factors. First, terrain and climate began to influence operations and tactics as early as autumn 1941. The same happened to the Panzer Divisions' shrinking fighting power, a consequence of the increasing losses and the lack of replacements. Tied as they were to the (few) major paved roads, the Panzer Divisions were no longer able to drive deeply into enemy territory as they had done the previous summer. Additionally, tracked elements such as the Panzer Regiment and the armoured infantry battalions not only took the lead, but, given their unique movement capabilities, soon turned into the only available units able to spearhead the attack. Attrition caused both by the enemy and the weather, unmatched by adequate reinforcements, eventually took its toll until Red Army counter-offensives of winter 1941/42 brought the first real change to the Panzer Divisions' tactics. Not only were the Panzer Divisions forced to fight on the defensive for the first time, but they also primarily had to do it with their non-armoured units since most of the armoured ones had practically ceased to exist as such.

German defensive tactics, based on the 'hold fast' principle (in which units facing an enemy attack had to maintain their positions regardless of what happened on their flanks and rear) coupled with the need to immediately counter-attack enemy breakthroughs, proved particularly suitable for the Panzer Divisions, though heavy losses further reduced their combat efficiency. This was never fully recovered, even after the reorganization of early 1942. Along with the Red Army's increased capabilities in defence, this produced a significant reduction to the Panzer Divisions' speed and manoeuvre capabilities. Balance in the two elements of the attack – fire and movement – significantly shifted in favour of fire. The main consequence was the inability to drive deeply into enemy territory, at least at a tactical level, plus the development of tighter command and control at every level. The Panzer Divisions, which were still superior to their opponents in the field, remained the spearhead of the German Army, but they no longer were able to assure breakthrough and the ensuing encirclement of enemy forces. Summer 1943, particularly the failure at Kursk, marked the turning point of the evolution of German armoured tactics which from that point turned the Panzer Divisions into 'fire-fighters'.

11. Panzer Division's drive to Dubno, 23–25 June 1941

The early stages of Operation *Barbarossa* were still ruled by blitzkrieg-style warfare. On 23 June 1941 XXXXVIII Panzer Korps started its drive to the 'Stalin' line, as part of Kleist's Panzergruppe 1 advance in the southern part of the Eastern Front. After infantry had broken through the Soviet border defences in the early morning of 23 June, 11. Panzer Division began its march with its Panzer Aufklärungs Abteilung in the lead. A few hours later it seized the village of Stojanow, opening the way to advance for other units. Panzer Regiment 15, in the lead, switched south toward the village of Radziechow, only to face a Soviet armoured brigade (part of the 15th Mechanized Corps) heading north. What followed was one of the first tank battles on the Eastern

Front, which lasted for about six hours and saw Panzer Regiment 15, supported by Schützen Regiment 111 and Artillerie Regiment 119, struggling to annihilate the Soviet threat. By midday Soviet forces were compelled to withdraw, having lost some 30 tanks, although German losses had also been high. This did not slow down the advance of the rest of the German division. Having taken the lead, Schützen Regiment 110 advanced toward Chmielno and, after a brief fight for control, moved on to Lypatin, which was taken without a struggle. At about the same time, Kradschützen Bataillon 61, which advanced north of the Styr River without encountering any serious enemy resistance, reached Merwa and Beresteczko and seized the bridges on the Styr intact. Panzer Regiment 15 established a small bridgehead and resumed its advance and, at 6.30 p.m., Schützen Regiment 110 reached Sczcurowjce only to find that the bridge had been destroyed. Nevertheless, small parties crossed the river.

At 7:00 a.m. on 24 June aerial reconnaissance reported large armoured enemy units to the south of 11. Panzer Division's line of advance to the west and the east of the Styr; their leading elements were already in the Brody area and moving toward Radziechow. To face the threat, elements of Panzer Regiment 15 and Schützen Regiment 111 were sent to the Lypatin area, but their advance was slowed by congestion on the roads and Soviet air raids. Meanwhile, both battalions of Schützen Regiment 110 formed a bridgehead to the east and the south of Sczcurowjce. 16. Panzer Division, part of XIV Panzer Korps, was sent after 11. Panzer Division on the road to Radziechow to help face the Soviet threat, but its advance was halted on roads blocked by Soviet support troops. Only Kradschützen Bataillon 61 was able to reconnoitre forward, seizing Ostrow in the morning. Late in the afternoon of 24 June, after Pionier Bataillon 209 had built a bridge at Sczcurowjce, 11. Panzer Division resumed its advance. At dusk the leading elements of I./Schützen Regiment 110 reconnoitred the road leading east, seizing Kozyn and reaching Plycza at night, which lay only 12km from Dubno. In the meantime Panzer Regiment 15 and Schützen Regiment 111 crossed the Styr and began their own advance, without waiting for 16. Panzer Division. At dawn on 25 June Schützen Regiment 110 attacked the enemy positions at Plycza and overcame them, opening the path for the further advance east. While the bulk of 11. Panzer Division massed to the south of Dubno, to the north Panzer Aufklärungs Abteilung 231 advanced toward Mlynow and seized it without a fight. The double pincer attack against Dubno started at 11:00 a.m., and the town was eventually seized shortly after 2:00 p.m. Meanwhile, forward elements of 16. Panzer Division reached the Chmielno area, ready to face the Soviet counter-attack.

11. Panzer Division's drive to
Dubno, 23–25 June 1941.

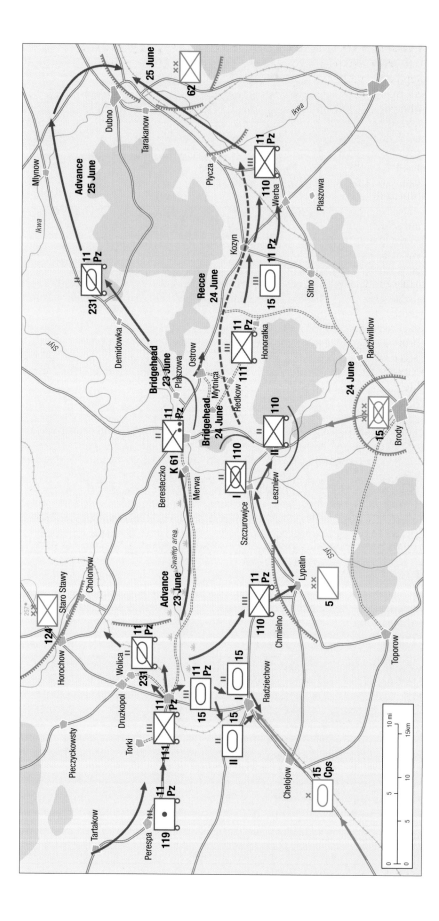

44

The Dvina River crossing, 7 July 1941

It is often assumed that German tactics only rarely required the use of firepower, an instrument otherwise preferred both by the Allies and the Soviets. As a matter of fact, the use of firepower was not unusual in the German Army, although at least in the first years of the war it was mainly restricted to circumstances such as the seizure of a fortress or the crossing of a river, such as at Sedan in May 1940. Also, firepower was mainly used to suppress enemy positions and prevent them from opening fire on advancing units. Therefore, in spite of the availability of armoured spotting vehicles for the Artillerie Regiment, the Panzer Divisions made extensive use of area fire, with their artillery firing on carefully preselected map coordinates.

During the Smolensk encirclement, 20. Panzer Division, spearheading Panzergruppe 3, advanced on the northern prong of the pincer, and eventually faced a major obstacle in its path: the Dvina River. Since the division had been slowed down by heavy rainfall, the Ic (intelligence officer) reported that Red Army units had had time to set up well-prepared defences (reinforced by artillery and anti-tank guns) on the north-eastern bank of the river, particularly in the area of Ulla. Having ruled out a surprise attack, the divisional commander Generalleutnant Horst Stumpff decided instead on an all-out attack with full fire support. Schützen Regiment 59 was to cross the Dvina north of Ulla, in the Komatschino area, following air attacks led by units of VIII Fliegerkorps, and after a 15-minute artillery bombardment performed by Artillerie Regiment 92 and other attached artillery units, including III. Abteilung of Nebelwerfer Regiment 51. As scheduled, the air bombardment

The Dvina River crossing, 7 July 1941.

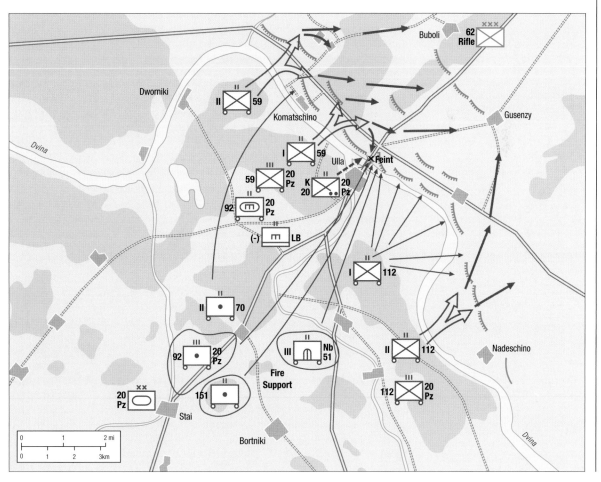

45

Two PzKpfw IIIs Ausf F, still armed with the 37mm gun, on a road in the Soviet Union during the early stages of *Barbarossa*. Both belong to the Kompanie Trupp of the seventh leichte Panzer Kompanie of an unknown unit. The PzKpfw II following them belongs to the leichte Panzer Zug of the same company.

began at 2:00 p.m. on 7 July 1941, followed 45 minutes later by the artillery one. Finally, at 3:00 p.m., the first assault boats of the Landungsboot Pionier Bataillon began to carry the Schützen across the river. The short but intense air bombardment and artillery fire succeeded in pinning down the enemy troops, who put up only scant resistance. With the enemy defences already distracted by the attack and under cover of direct fire from I./Schützen Regiment 112, men of II./SR 112 crossed the Dvina north of Nadeschino, where the enemy defences stood far from the riverbank. In the meantime Kradschützen Bataillon 20 carried out a feint attack at Ulla. Soon the men of the Soviet 62nd Rifle Division reorganized and started to fire on the two battalions of Schützen Regiment 59, which had already crossed the river. Schützen Regiment 112 faced only light resistance, which enabled it to bring its heavy weapons across the river. At 4:50 p.m. Komatschino fell into German hands, while to the south, Schützen Regiment 112 advanced to the main road. Eventually Schützen Regiment 59 attacked the bridge area of Ulla at 7:30 p.m., seizing it shortly thereafter. Its success cost 200 killed and wounded. Bridging elements of Panzer Pionier Bataillon 92 began erecting a bridge over the river, which was opened at 9:00 a.m. on 8 July. Two minutes later the leading elements of the division began their advance to Vitebsk, which 20. Panzer Division seized in the afternoon of 9 July.

The raid across the Susha River, 23–24 October 1941

On 30 October 1941 Guderian's Panzergruppe 2 started the new offensive toward Moscow, Operation *Typhoon*. In spite of initial success, it was soon clear that conditions now were quite different to how they had been during the summer of Operation *Barbarossa*. Attrition and lack of replacements reduced the Panzer Divisions' operational effectiveness and, at the beginning of *Typhoon*, Guderian's units were left with only half the number of serviceable tanks of their establishment; problems also arose because of the ever-growing supply shortages. Lastly, the rain and snowfalls that began in the first week of October soon turned every road, with the exception of the few paved ones, into mires in which only tracked vehicles could move. Under such conditions, in mid-October XXIV Panzer Korps began to prepare for the crossing of the Susha River (a major waterway, up to 40m wide) in the Msensk area, to the north of Orel and on the road to Tula. 4. Panzer Division, reinforced by the 'Grossdeutschland' motorized infantry regiment, was to attack Msensk along the major road, which was heavily defended and blocked. Thus, the main effort switched to 3. Panzer Division, which was to cross the river just to the north of Msensk to outflank Soviet defences. For this purpose two special battle groups were formed: the major one was Kampfgruppe Eberbach, led by Oberst Heinrich Eberbach and formed around the HQ of Panzer Brigade 5 with its three Panzer Abteilungen, the I./Schützen Regiment 3 and I./SR 394 plus Panzer Pionier Bataillon 39 and artillery support. The southern attack group was formed around the HQ of Schützen Brigade 3 and included II./SR 3 and II./SR 394. Actual strength was quite low, with each Panzer Abteilung having only 20–25 serviceable tanks. Road conditions urged Eberbach on to ingenuity; since trucks were unable to move forward in such terrain, he ordered that one half-tracked prime mover loaded with 1,500 litres of fuel had to be attached to every Abteilung, while another one carrying 6,000 litres in a trailer was to follow his Kampfgruppe.

During the night of 22/23 October, the southern attack group moved first. Shortly after midnight the II./SR 3 started to cross the river on the bend to the north of Msensk. The crossing was completed by 5:30 a.m., when the battalion turned the small bridgehead into a defensive position. An artillery barrage hammered the Kampfgruppe Eberbach crossing area at 6:00 a.m. Shortly thereafter the I./SR 3 began to cross the river just south of Roshenez. Enemy positions were overrun, and the battalion turned south, toward Nikolskaya. Under heavy artillery fire (including German artillery fire), it was soon compelled to halt its advance and to seek cover until the Panzers arrived. However, to the north, II./SR 394 encountered many problems while crossing the river and was only able to establish a bridgehead in the late afternoon. Panzer Pionier Bataillon 39 began building a bridge at a suitable crossing point of the Susha River, where the two floating sections (each 10m wide and weighing 16 tons) of the bridge were laid under heavy enemy artillery fire. The bridge was opened four hours later than expected, at 9.30 a.m. on 24 October, and immediately III./Panzer Regiment 6 got across the river along with 1. Kompanie of Schützen Regiment 3 on its Schützenpanzerwagen, followed by I./SR 394, which secured the bridgehead. Road conditions further delayed the Panzers; only by midday did III./PzRgt 6 move east toward Shalamowo, while I./PzRgt 6, the second to get across the Susha, switched south to Nikolskaya. It attacked to the south with I./SR 3, and by 4:00 p.m. contact was established with II./SR 3. The reorganized Kampfgruppe then moved south-east towards Katuschischtscha to reach III./Infanterie Regiment 'Grossdeutschland', which attacked enemy positions in front of Msensk. However, the Soviet defences prevented them from achieving their objective. At Shalamowo III./PzRgt 6 encountered a group of seven Soviet T-34s; after a brief clash two of these were destroyed at the cost of two PzKpfw III. Eventually the Soviet tanks pulled out, and the first elements of II./PzRgt 6 joined III. Abteilung, bringing more badly needed fuel canisters. After a heavy Stuka attack, the two Panzer Abteilungen resumed their advance in late afternoon and at nightfall seized both Mal Borsenski and Manewa, facing only slight enemy resistance. Eberbach then decided to exploit the situation: III./PzRgt 6 and 1.Kp./SR 3 set up a night raid on Whs, the depot and maintenance area of the Soviet 11th Armoured Brigade. The fight was once more brief and ferocious; it was over by midnight, when Kampfgruppe Eberbach seized its final target. The enemy defences had been penetrated, and the road to Tula was open.

The advance of a reconnaissance column, either from a Panzer Aufklärungs Abteilung or a Kradschützen Bataillon, is temporarily halted by the crater made during a Stuka attack that has disabled the Soviet tank in the foreground. Air support was essential to the speedy advance of the Panzer Divisions – although in this case it has inadvertently caused something of a hindrance.

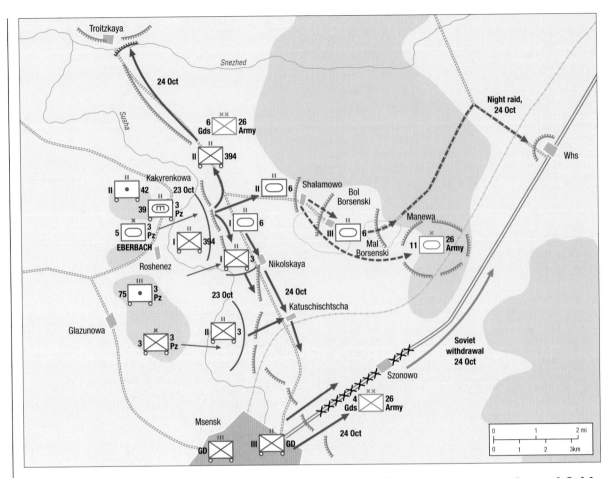

The raid across the Susha River, 23–24 October 1941.

Counter-attack at Klin, 11 December 1941

The Soviet counter-offensive unleashed on 5 December 1941 clearly marked the end of the blitzkrieg era for the Panzer Divisions. Already depleted and understrength, for the very first time they were now forced to defend against a major enemy offensive, and not just counter-attacks as they had done to date. This time, the fight was for their own survival. To the north-west of Moscow, Panzergruppe 3 faced a difficult situation, given the threat of being outflanked to the north by advancing Soviet units. The German units withdrew, but the Red Army forces arrived faster than expected. To meet the threat from the Soviet 30th Army, on 10 December 1. Panzer Division established a series of Sperrverbände (blocking formations) around Klin. Kampfgruppe Westhoven, formed by remnants of Schützen Regiment 1, defended the area north of Gubino; however, it was in the process of being relieved by 14. Infanterie Division (motorisiert), and was about to redeploy to Teterino where it would take under its command II./SR 113 and I./SR 2 from 2. Panzer Division. Gruppe Knopff, the bulk made up of Pionier Bataillon 630 and Panzer Pionier Bataillon 37 plus elements from both 1 and 2. Panzer Divisions, was deployed to the south-west and joined with Gruppe Kopp, which included the remnants of Panzer Regiment 25 and elements from the two Panzer Divisions. The only operational reserve left to the division was Kampfgruppe Wietersheim, formed from the Kradschützen Bataillon 1 plus I./SR 113 (Bataillon Krieg, equipped with all the remaining Schützen Panzerwagen) and I./PzRgt 1, the so-called Abteilung Grampe which had been formed from the merger of the remaining Panzers of Panzer Regiment 1 with those of the Panzer-Flammenwerfer (flame-thrower) Abteilung 101. On 10 December the Sperrverbände successfully

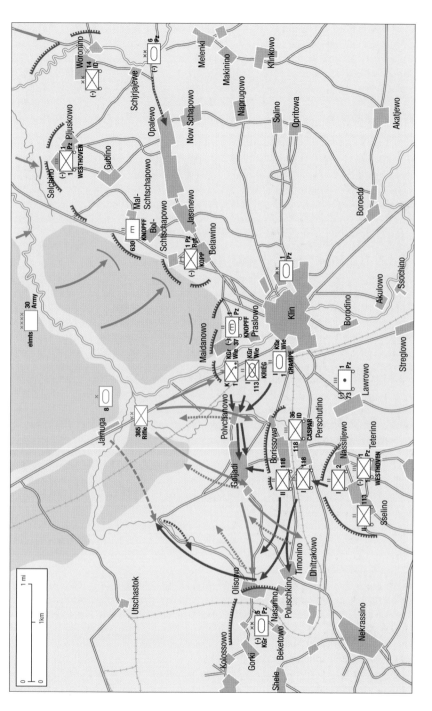

repulsed the Soviet advances to the east of Klin, but the threat to the west – and to the escape route for the bulk of Panzergruppe 3 – also became clear. In the afternoon the Soviet 365th Rifle Division seized the villages of Poluchanowo and Goljadi; its spearheads threatened Borissowo and successfully cut the road to the west between there and Timonino.

Faced by this situation, 1. Panzer Division organized a counter-attack for the next day. Kampfgruppe Wietersheim gathered north of Klin while Kampfgruppe Caspar of 36. Infanterie Division (mot) was deployed at Borissowo (which it was to hold at all costs) to make up for the absence of Kampfgruppe Westhoven, which had been unable to redeploy because of the enemy's attack. Though delayed by a lack of supplies, Kampfgruppe Wietersheim started its attack at 9:00 a.m. and surrounded Poluchanowo, destroying all enemy forces there. Progress made by Kampfgruppe Caspar was slower, though at 11:00 a.m. it reached Timonino and pushed back the Soviet spearheads, eventually re-establishing contact with the easternmost elements of 5. Panzer Division. Meanwhile, I./SR 2 (placed under temporary command of Kampfgruppe Caspar) advanced north toward Goljadi to meet up with Kampfgruppe Wietersheim and its spearhead, Bataillon Krieg. Goljadi was seized at 11:15 a.m., though Oberstleutnant Krieg had to give up any further advance westwards due to his men's exhaustion and the lack of supplies. However, since the counter-attack had clearly succeeded, the divisional commander, Generalmajor Krüger, ordered Kampfgruppe Caspar to continue its attack toward Jamuga, which Oberst Caspar did at 2:45 a.m. – only to be brought to a halt shortly afterwards. Faced by strong Soviet defences and an enemy armoured thrust, he eventually withdrew.

The battle for Charkow, 16–20 May 1942

Although replenished and reorganized after the winter battles, by spring 1942 the Panzer Divisions possessed only part of the fighting power they had had just one year before. Shortages of vehicles, tanks and equipment were only part of the problem. More seriously, the Panzer Divisions were affected by the lack of suitable replacements and especially of experienced officers. As a result they lacked the capability to move fast and to drive deep into enemy-held territory. On 12 May 1942, when the Soviet offensive against Charkow began, both 3 and 23. Panzer Divisions were still feeling their winter losses. Nevertheless, they were redeployed and put into defence east of Charkow, with orders to prepare to counter-attack east to relieve Kampfgruppe Gruner of 168. Infanterie Division, which had been surrounded at Ternowaja. 3. Panzer Division put together a Kampfgruppe under the command of Oberstleutnant Schmidt-Ott made up of III./Panzer Regiment 6 and I./Schützen Regiment 3, supported by 3. Kompanie of Panzer Pionier Bataillon 39 and 1. Batterie of Artillerie Regiment 75. The following day Kampfgruppe Schmidt-Ott moved north-east and started its counter-attack, eventually seizing Nepokrytaja. It was soon relieved by a Kampfgruppe of 23. Panzer Division, made up of I./PzRgt 201 and I./SR 126, and it switched its route to the north-west to attack Wesseloje. Although personally wounded, and facing strong Soviet resistance, Schmidt-Ott seized his objective while the advance of 23. Panzer Division's Kampfgruppe was halted at Peremoga, north of Nepokrytaja.

A renewed effort was requested from both of them on 16 May, with Kampfgruppe Schmidt-Ott attacking north-east towards Ternowaja and the Kampfgruppe of 23. Panzer Division attacking north towards Peremoga. Other units, including 71 and 294. Infanterie Divisions, the latter having been attached to Kampfgruppe Zimmermann (3. Panzer Division's Schützen Regiment 394), plus 23. Panzer Division's II./PzRgt 201 and II./Schützen Regiment 3 – which joined Kampfgruppe Schmidt-Ott – were brought in. The attack was initially successful to the east and to the north-east of Wesseloje; II./SR 3 quickly seized Neskutschnoje, capturing more than 700 Soviet soldiers, but I./SR 3 and III./PzRgt 6 faced stiff opposition, and their advance was soon brought to a halt. Likewise, 23. Panzer Division's attack toward Peremoga faced strong enemy resistance, and the Kampfgruppe had to switch its axis of advance to the north-west. Soviet counter-attacks, supported by large numbers of tanks, were dealt with by air support from Stuka Gruppe 77, although the price was high. Both Kampfgruppe Schmidt-Ott and 23. Panzer Division closed in on hill 200.9, which was eventually seized on 19 May.

At this point 23. Panzer Division took command of both Kampfgruppen. Its commander, Generalmajor Erwin Mack, ordered Schmidt-Ott to advance the following day toward Ternowaja. The attack started in the morning of 20 May, and soon came face to face with a Soviet tank counter-attack; this was dealt with by III./PzRgt 6, which destroyed six T-34s. Soon after, the Stukas arrived, spreading havoc amongst the enemy forces. The follow-up Schützen fought hard to overcome the Soviet defences and suffered heavy losses, including many officers, and in late morning the Red Army troops began to collapse. With a *coup de main*, III./PzRgt 6 seized hill 208.7, where the regiment refuelled and replenished. At dusk its spearheads reached hill 219.7; the encirclement around Ternowaja was finally broken at 10:00 a.m. the following day.

Defence at Belyj, 30 November 1942

There were two elements to German defensive doctrine: 'hold fast' and counter-attack. The purpose of the 'hold fast' was to shatter the enemy attack and isolate its spearheads. Direct, prompt counter-attacks were also required to halt enemy breakthroughs and to restore the defence line by linking up with the units left behind that otherwise would be encircled and annihilated. Needless to say, this tactic required strong nerves and determination: even a single mistake might lead to disaster.

While this tactic failed badly at Stalingrad, it proved effective during the Soviet offensive against the Rzhev salient, held by Heeresgruppe Mitte (Army Group Centre), which was launched on 25 November 1942. On its western side, Soviet 41st Army units managed to break through the German defences south of Belyj, advancing deep into the German-held front. However, not only did they fail to seize Belyj, defended by 1. Panzer Division's Kampfgruppe Kruger – which included Panzergrenadier Regiment 113 (Kampfgruppe von Wietersheim, with the bulk of II./SR 113, I./Panzer Regiment 33 from 9. Panzer Division and II./Artillerie Regiment 73), along with two Kampfgruppen from 246. Infanterie Division and 10. Infanterie Division (mot) plus the Füsilier Regiment 'Grossdeutschland' – but they also faced stubborn resistance from other elements of 1. Panzer Division. To face the Soviet breakthrough, Kampfgruppe von der Meden was deployed on the eastern bank of the Natscha River. Under the command of Panzergrenadier Regiment 1, it included II./PzRgt 1 (the only tank unit with 1. Panzer Division), I and II./PzGrenRgt 1 and the Kradschützen Bataillon 1. Gruppe Holste, including Panzerjäger Abteilung 37 and Panzer Pionier Bataillon 37, deployed to the south to defend the vital town of Wladimirskoje. These units were to hold their positions until the relief force, made up of 12, 19 and 20. Panzer Divisions, dealt with the enemy breakthrough and restored the defence line. Although the attack by the 41st Soviet Army focused on Belyj, its 1st Mechanized Corps pressed on, and by 27 November had managed to cross the Natscha River in several places to the north and the south of Bossino. Only the stubborness of Kampfgruppe von der Meden's units, most notably of Kradschützen Bataillon 1, prevented an enemy breakthrough and complete disaster. However, Kampfgruppe von der Meden's defence line was broken into two; from now on the northern group at Stepankowa could only be supplied via a path opened across the woods. The German situation worsened on 28 November when a new Soviet attack south-east of Belyj broke through the defences and opened the way to the Soviet 47th Mechanized Brigade's drive north.

The stubborn defence put up by the Germans and a slowing in the Soviet attack (particularly with the decision to focus on Belyj) prevented outright disaster, but the German situation gravely worsened. Between 29 and 30 November the gap between Kampfgruppe Kruger at Belyj and Kampfgruppe von der Meden widened, allowing the Soviet 47th Mechanized Brigade to advance north to the Otscha River, before eventually being halted by the Kradschützen Bataillon 'Grossdeutschland'. To the east, the German front disintegrated, leaving only a series of strongpoints that the Soviets could apparently overrun at will. On 30 November a decisive attack was launched by the Soviet 1st Mechanized Corps. In the morning, following a heavy snowfall,

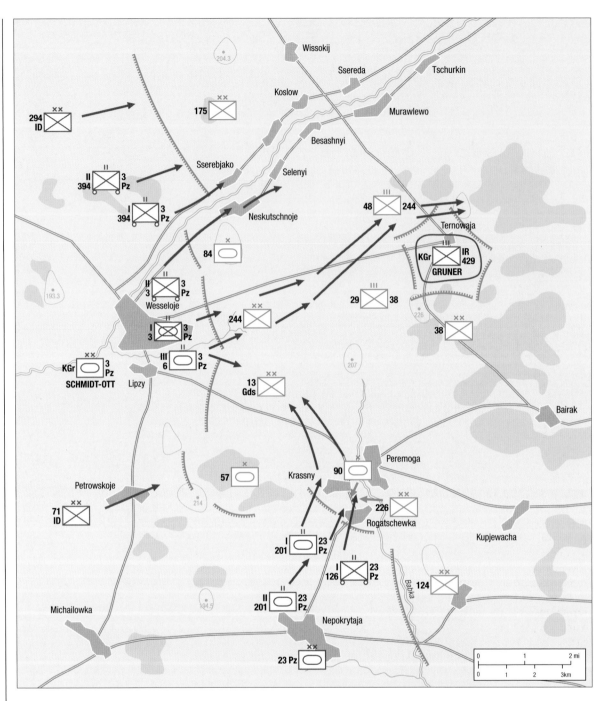

The Battle for Charkow, 16–20 May 1942.

219th and 65th Tank Brigades supported by 78th Rifle Brigade pressed on across the bridgehead on the Natscha against the positions held by II./PzRgt 1 and I./PzGrenRgt 1, their leading units pushing through the German lines as far as Smoljano. In the meantime, the 35th Mechanized Brigade advancing from the south threatened to encircle Kampfgruppe von der Meden's northernmost units. However, the Soviet advance was hindered there by Kradschützen Bataillon 1, which was encircled at Petelino after its attempt to re-establish contact between the northern and the southern elements of Kampfgruppe von der Meden. Even the attempt to wipe out the southern group led by part of the 35th and the entire 37th Soviet Mechanized Brigades plus the

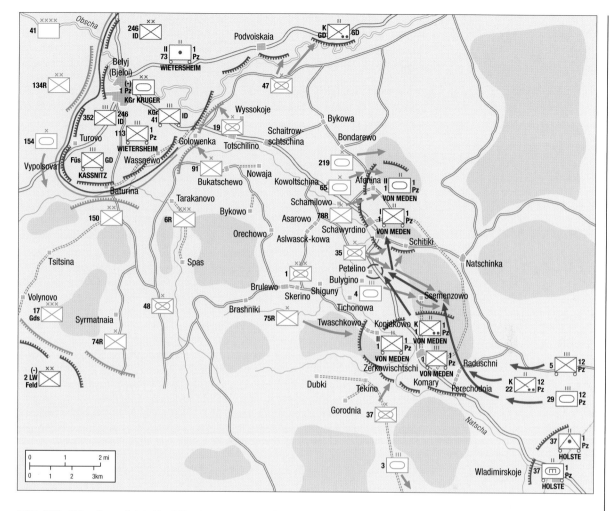

Defence at Belyj,
30 November 1942.

75th Rifle Brigade and 4th Tank Regiment eventually failed, simply because the German defenders clung to their positions and fought to the last. In four days of combat, II./PzRgt 1 destroyed more than 40 Soviet tanks, and by 30 November it still had two PzKpfw III operational. Although desperate, the German situation was not hopeless. By mid-afternoon the leading elements of 12. Panzer Division joined Kampfgruppe von der Meden's southern group and counter-attacked the Soviet spearheads at Ssemenzowo, pushing on to Petelino to relieve the encircled Kradschützen Bataillon 1 and eventually linking up with I./PzGrenRgt 1 before nightfall. The Soviet 1st Mechanized Corps switched to the defensive, now aware that the opportunity had been lost and that the German front was going to be restored.

The drive on Stalingrad, 18–19 December 1942

It was during winter 1942/43 that the Panzer Divisions were first used as 'fire fighters' – units tasked with restoring the defensive line and counter-attacking the enemy following an enemy breakthrough. All too often, they were called upon to perform this role despite their reduced combat power and poor state of readiness.

Operation *Wintergewitter* (winter storm), launched by LVII Panzer Korps on 12 December in an attempt to relieve the forces encircled at Stalingrad, involved three Panzer Divisions (6 and 23, plus 17 from 16 December) giving a joint combat strength of about 17,000 men and about 200 tanks. In particular, the lack of modern tanks greatly affected the Panzer Divisions' fighting power.

The actual tank strength of the three divisions on the evening of 18 December was: 6. Panzer Division – 38 PzKpfw III and five PzKpfw in running order; 17. Panzer Division – 30 PzKpfw III and 14 PzKpfw IV; and 23. Panzer Division – eight PzKpfw III and six PzKpfw IV (giving a grand total of 101 tanks). During nine days of combat between 12 and 20 December, 6. Panzer Division had 25 tanks written off, 17. Panzer Division had 20 tanks undergoing minor repairs and 23. Panzer Division had eight write-offs. The three divisions also had 83 tanks undergoing major repairs. (The difference between this total of 156 and the above-listed 101 is accounted for by the 55 tanks lost between 18 and 20 December). Facing these figures and the enemy's ever-growing strength, by late 1942 the Panzer Divisions were clearly no longer capable of dealing with attritional warfare and of maintaining their combat capabilities. It was possible in 1940 and in 1941, when the Panzer Divisions inflicted heavy losses on the enemy that counterbalanced their own reduced capabilities, but in late 1942 the days of such rapid advances were over.

In three days of combat, 6. Panzer Division advanced more than 70km, established a bridgehead on the Akssaij River at Saliwiskij and pushed forward to Werchne Kumskij, where it met strong enemy resistance that prevented any further advance. By 17 December sustained combat had caused many losses, including tanks that could not be recovered due to the lack of equipment, and brought exhaustion to the troops. The divisional combat units had been arranged as follows. The leading element was Kampfgruppe Hünersdorff formed by Panzer Regiment 11 (two companies of which had been detached to Kampfgruppe Zollenkopf) plus the Schützen Panzerwagen-mounted II./PzGrenRgt 114, most of the Panzer Pionier Bataillon 57 and elements of the Panzerjäger Abteilung 41. Supporting it was Kampfgruppe Zollenkopf, made up of I./PzGrenRgt 4 and I./PzGrenRgt 114 supported by I./Artillerie Regiment 76 and most of Panzerjäger Abteilung 41. Kradschützen Bataillon 6 formed Kampfgruppe Quentin, while the Stab of Panzergrenadier Regiment 4 formed Kampfgruppe Unrein, with II./PzGrenRgt 4 at its disposal. Thanks to the arrival of 17. Panzer Division's lead units, which established their own bridgehead at Nowo Aksaisskij, Kampfgruppe Zollendorf could be reunited and used for a renewed attack against Werchne Kumskij. The attack of Kampfgruppe Zollenkopf, supported by two Panzer Kompanien plus Kampfgruppe Quentin, was unable to break through the enemy defences; by midday the two Panzer Kompanien were left with two serviceable tanks, and at dusk the attack was called off. It would be renewed the following day with a three-pronged attack from 17. Panzer Division and Kampfgruppen Zollenkopf and Hünersdorff, the latter also tasked with immediately advancing north after the seizure of Werchne Kumskij, regardless of the need to secure its flanks.

The leading element of 17. Panzer Division was Kampfgruppe Seitz, made up of Panzergrenadier Regiment 63 supported by one Panzerjäger and one Pionier Kompanie plus one artillery battalion. It began to advance towards a kolchos (collective farm) on 8 March, though supporting tanks (II./PzRgt 39) were slowed down and arrived late. Combat around the kolchos lasted for the entire day against stubborn defence and the threat of counter-attacks. At 5:00 a.m. on 19 December the two Panzer Divisions resumed their attacks against the Soviet defences in and around the kolchos and Werchne Kumskij. This time the joint effort, along with air support, seized the two enemy-held positions by 11:00 a.m., though it did not lead to a breakthrough. 17. Panzer Division was ordered to advance north, while Kampfgruppe Hünersdorff, after a brief advance north to hill 114, was ordered to turn east and head towards the road junction at hill 146.9,

Even tracked vehicles in the Panzer Divisions had a tough time trying to keep moving in the mud and mires encountered in the Soviet Union.

in part because of a Soviet counter-attack against 23. Panzer Division's bridgehead. During the afternoon there were two German drives forward: one by 17. Panzer Division to the north, which eventually seized Nizne Kumskij at dusk, and another one to the west by Kampfgruppe Hünersdorff, whose advance was halted at 3:00 p.m. by strong enemy defences around hill 146.9. Reinforced by I./PzGrenRgt 4, Hünersdorff switched south and succeeded in breaking through the enemy defences about an hour later. In the winter darkness Kampfgruppe Hünersdorff set off, following a track to Gnilo Aksaiskaja, avoiding enemy defences there and then switching north, eventually crossing the bridge at Wassiljewka on the Muschkova River at 10:00 p.m. after a 30km march – only to meet the enemy defences made up of the leading elements of

A PzKpfw III of 11. Panzer Division – the Gespenst ('ghost') insignia is just visible on the left side – moving on a snow-covered road during the winter of 1941/42. The German Army's lack of preparation for the Soviet winter was due to the common belief that the campaign would be over within a few months.

the Soviet 4th Guards Army. This day marked the northernmost advance of LVII Panzer Korps' Operation *Wintergewitter*, which would last for only two more days, having reached a position 48km away from the Stalingrad pocket.

Last battle at Rostow, 13 February 1943

The German withdrawal from the Stalingrad area back to the Donets River line between December 1942 and January 1943 clearly showed the capabilities of the Panzer Divisions. For three weeks 4. Panzerarmee's units pulled back to Rostow and the southern Donets bend – a distance of 350km – while facing Red Army attacks that threatened to cut off their lines of retreat. Quite remarkably, the divisions of LVII Panzer Korps, already depleted after the ill-fated Operation *Wintergewitter*, managed to deal with this difficult situation by quickly redeploying and, in spite of their reduced fighting power, using small-scale counter-attacks, enabling the Germans to gain a temporary edge over the enemy. In the fluid situation created by the enemy offensive, blitzkrieg concepts would again prove successful, even though this time they were used in a mobile defence.

At the beginning of February 1943, 4. Panzerarmee LVII entrusted Panzer Korps with the task of defending the city of Rostow against the enemy offensive, which threatened to cut the retreat of German forces south and inside the Donets River bend line. The defence of Rostow fell into the hands of what was left of the Kampfgruppe of 23. Panzer Division after one and one-half months of fighting. By then the actual strength of Panzer Regiment 201 (now practically reduced to its I. Abteilung only) was about 20 tanks – those that had been heavily damaged and recovered during the early stages of *Wintergewitter* and had been returned to the division after a long period of repair. Even schwere Panzer Abteilung 503, which had been attached to 23. Panzer Division in January, was in not much better shape; by mid-February it had only two Tigers and eight PzKpfw III operational out of the 17 Tigers and 20 PzKpfw III of early January.

The first Soviet attempt to establish a bridgehead on the Donets River was made on 8 February 1943 just to the west of the Donets–Don watersmeet, at Ssemernikowo. A counter-attack was immediately launched using II./Panzergrenadier Regiment 128, which, supported by Panzer Regiment 201 and schwere Panzer Abteilung 503, prevented a breakthrough. A renewed, full-scale Soviet attempt started on 12 February, this time to the east of Kalinin Chapry. Since the area was defended only by the weak 444. Sicherungs Division (security division, intended for use in a rear-area security role), the bridgehead soon turned into a breakthrough aimed to the north, against the Sapadnyi station and the Rostow–Tschaltyr road. Immediately, both Panzer Regiment 201 and schwere Panzer Abteilung 503 were sent to the Sapadnyi station area

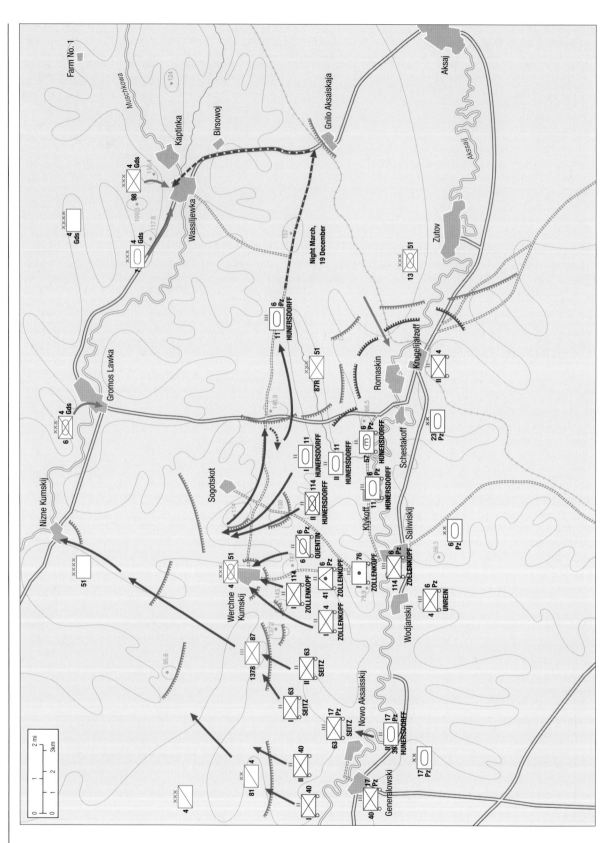

The drive towards Stalingrad, 18–19 December 1942.

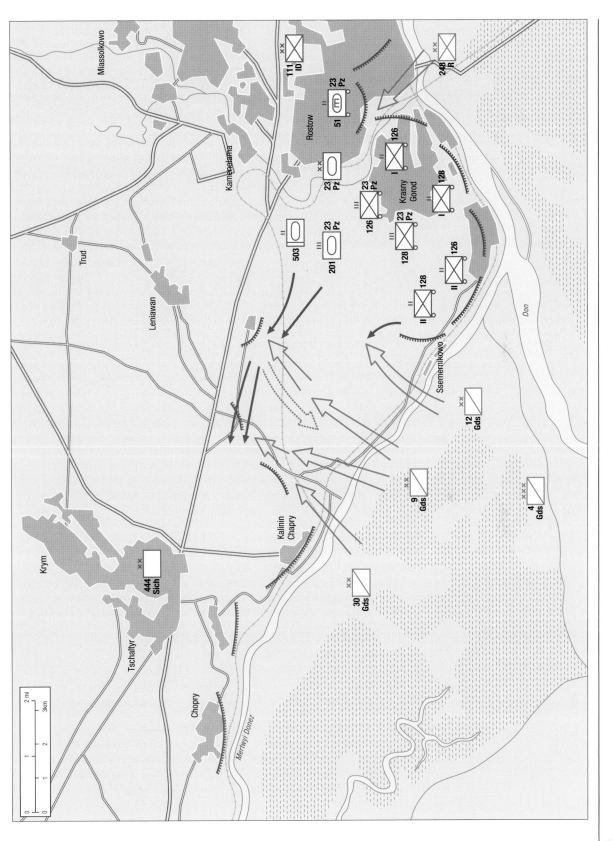

The last battle at Rostow, 13 February 1943.

An SdKfz 7 prime mover hauls a 150mm schwere Feldhaubitze 18 (heavy howitzer) through deep snow. Despite being the only equipment capable of movement in the harsh conditions experienced on the Eastern Front, towed artillery could not meet the rapid movement requirements of the Panzer Divisions.

to prevent the enemy breakthrough, which eventually did happen. However, the time had come to abandon these untenable positions; at 9:00 a.m. on 13 February, LVII Panzer Korps was ordered to get ready to withdraw north, leaving behind only 23. Panzer Division and 16. Infanterie Division (mot) to act as rearguards. On the same morning, Soviet forces attacked again; at Rostow the 248th Rifle Division established a bridgehead between Rostow and the Krasny Gorod suburb, while 12th Cavalry Division attacked from the west against II./PzGrenRgt 128 and, further west, 30 and 9th Cavalry Division (all with tanks support) pressed north. While German infantry and engineers successfully defended their positions in house-to-house fighting, Panzer Regiment 201 and schwere Panzer Abteilung 503 attacked to the west and prevented the enemy breakthrough from getting farther north. The withdrawal started at 8:00 p.m. under cover of darkness; all the bridges still left were destroyed and both Panzergrenadier Regiments extricated themselves from a difficult situation and redeployed just to the north of Rostow on a new, temporary defensive line. A few days later 23. Panzer Division was pulled out from the front to rest and refit.

III Panzer Korps at Kursk, 11–12 July 1943

On the right wing of Heeresgruppe Süd's offensive against the Kursk salient during Operation *Zitadelle*, III Panzer Korps faced a hard, two-fold task: on one hand it was to defend the eastern side of the offensive from Soviet counter-attacks and, on the other, it was to support the main attack towards Prokhorovka by threatening to envelop the latter's defences from the right. These tasks were not easy, especially because – contrary to the blitzkrieg concept – the attack was aimed against well-prepared and defended enemy positions. Once more the Panzer Divisions were to rely on firepower rather than on manoeuvre to break through the enemy defences which, in this instance, were not only strong but also echeloned in depth.

During five days of hard fighting, III Panzer Korps' units – 19, 6 and 7. Panzer Divisions – slowly fought their way into the enemy defences to the east of Belgorod. By 10 July, 6. Panzer Division's advance was stalled north of Melechowo, while 19. Panzer Division cleared the enemy positions east of the Donets and 7. Panzer Division protected the eastern flank of the drive. In a last attempt to break the stalemate, an attack was launched on 11 July with the aim of breaking through the enemy positions and establishing a bridgehead on the Donets, from where the Soviet forces west of the river could be threatened by encirclement against the right wing of 4. Panzerarmee's front. However, the task was not going to be easy given the Panzer Divsions' losses, due both to enemy fire and attrition. On 11 July, 6. Panzer Division's II./Panzer Regiment 11 still had some 40 PzKpfw III and IV out of the roughly 100 at its disposal on 6 July when *Zitadelle* was launched. (The schwere Panzer Abteilung, attached to the division, had 19 Tiger tanks.) 19. Panzer Division was in even worse shape but, to make up for its losses, Grenadier Regiment 429 from 198. Infanterie Division was attached to it.

At dawn on 11 July, II./PzRgt 11 and schwere Panzer Abteilung 503 (forming Kampfgruppe von Oppeln-Bronikowski) moved north to attack Olchowatka, their advance slowed down by Soviet artillery fire, well concealed anti-tank guns and extended minefields. With the Tiger tanks leading the way, the German Panzer drive managed to approach Olchowatka, which was seized after meeting little enemy resistance. Then, 6. Panzer Division's tanks drove north towards Werchnij Olchonez while II./Panzergrenadier Regiment 4 joined them. Later in the morning they broke through the defences of the Soviet 107th Rifle Division, eventually enabling the Panzergrenadiers to push further on and seize the village of Kasatschje at dusk, where Kampfgruppe von Oppeln-Bronikowski would join them at 10:00 p.m. The way to the drive towards the northern Donets had been opened, yet that would only have been of use if 19. Panzer Division succeeded in securing the left flank of the drive. At 9.30 a.m. leading elements of the division (still fighting to the south) leapt forward to attack the village of Kisseljowo; the attack group, which included Panzergrenadier Regiment 73 and 74 plus Grenadier 429 and Panzer Aufklärungs Abteilung 19, advanced towards Kisseljowo, initially without meeting enemy resistance but drawing heavy artillery fire. Resistance suddenly manifested itself at the very outskirts of the village, which was eventually seized later in the morning. From there, 19. Panzer Division, supported by elements of 168. Infanterie Division, advanced north towards Ssabynino on the eastern bank of the Donets. The attack started at 7:45 a.m. on 12 July with Panzergrenadier Regiment 73 moving from Kisseljowo, while Panzer Aufklärungs Abteilung 19 and Panzergrenadier Regiment 74, supported by Panzer Regiment 27, tried to outflank the village. Grenadier Regiment 442, which moved north to Werchnij Olchonez, followed the road opened by 6. Panzer Division's advance trying to break the Soviet defences on the east. Once more heavy Soviet artillery fire, concealed anti-tank guns and tanks provided a formidable hurdle, which was eventually overcome by the Germans. By midday Ssabynino had been seized.

PzKpfw IIIs of 24. Panzer Division advancing through the streets of Voronesh in July 1942; the divisional insignia is visible on the right of the tanks. In summer 1942 new camouflage was introduced to German tanks and AFVs, comprising green mottling sprayed over the standard *Panzergrau* (tank grey).

The previous night, the extraordinary exploits of Kampfgruppe von Oppeln-Bronikowski had already assured III Panzer Korps' success. At midnight the reinforced Kampfgruppe set off for its final objective, the village of Rshawez on the Donets. The way was led by two captured Soviet T-34 tanks, after which followed a mixed column made up of II./PzRgt 11 and the Schützen Panzerwagen-mounted II./PzGrenRgt 114, with schwere Panzer Abteilung 503 at the rear. During a four-hour march into the darkness of a moonless night, the Kampfgruppe approached Rshawez, eluding Soviet troops and marching columns. Moving out of the night unseen, they stormed the Red Army positions inside Rshawez, destroying several tanks and other vehicles in a short, fierce battle that, however, did not prevent the eventual destruction of the bridge. Rshawez was seized and, with the enemy front already broken, I./PzGrenRgt 114 was sent north from Kasatschje (where it protected the right wing of the German drive along with II./PzGrenRgt 4) and was used to establish a bridgehead on the Donets in the early morning of 12 July. Later that same day, 19. Panzer Division's units, after the seizure of Ssabynino, advanced north, seizing Kriwzowo and Strelnikoff to eventually link up with Kampfgruppe von Oppeln-Bronikowski at 2:45 p.m. III Panzer Korps had attained its goal and was now only some 15km from Prokhorovka, but the worst had not yet come: Red Army units began to press on both relatively weak flanks of the German drive (at Schljachowo Panzer Aufklärungs Abteilung 6 still held 6. Panzer Division's right flank waiting for relief from the 7. Panzer Division, which did not arrive) while from the north, the Soviet Group Trufanov, which included two Guards Mechanized Brigades, attacked Kampfgruppe von Oppeln-Bronikowski's positions at Rshawez and at the bridgehead on the Donets. On 13 July the bridgehead was expanded and 19. Panzer Division relieved the shattered elements of 6. Panzer Division, now left with only 14 operational tanks. III Panzer Korps' drive from the Rshawez bridgehead continued and, eventually, on 16 July, the Soviet forces to the west of the Donets withdrew, allowing for the final link up with II SS Panzer Korps. That same day a major Soviet counter-offensive was started and *Zitadelle* was called off.

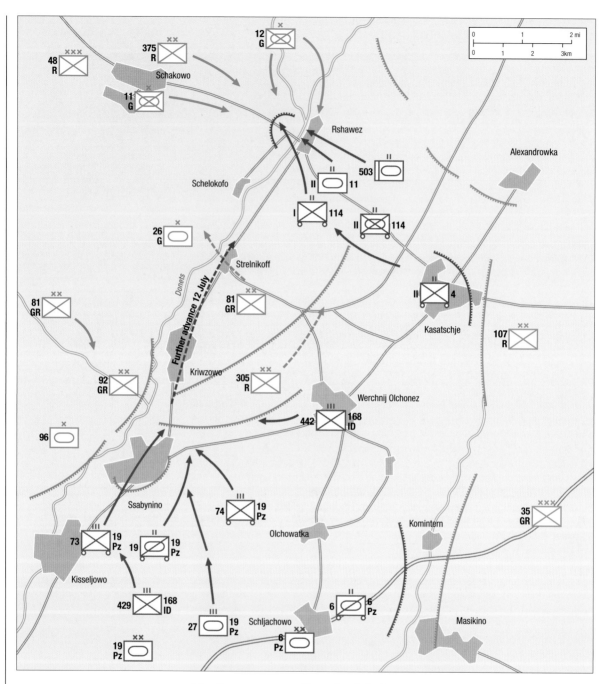

48
R
×××

375
R
××

12
G
×

Schakowo

11
G
×

Rshawez

Alexandrowka

503
ll

Schelokofo

ll
11

26
G
×

I
ll
114

ll
114

II
ll
4

81
GR
××

Strelnikoff

81
GR
××

Kasatschje

107
R
××

92
GR
××

Kriwzowo

305
R
×

Werchnij Olchonez

96
×

442

168
ID
lll

Donets

Further advance 12 July

Ssabynino

74
lll

19
Pz

Olchowatka

35
GR
×××

73
lll

19
Pz

19
ll

19
Pz

Komintern

Kisseljowo

429
lll

168
ID

27
lll

19
Pz

Schljachowo

6
ll

6
Pz

Masikino

19
Pz
××

6
Pz
××

III Panzer Korps at Kursk,
11–12 July 1943.

Defence at Orel, 16 July 1943

The end of *Zitadelle* marked the end of an era, that of the German offensives spearheaded by the Panzer Divisions. Not until December 1944 would the Panzer Divisions launch a major offensive; instead, they fought on the defensive, or, at best, in minor and tactical counter-offensive operations.

On 12 July 1943 the Soviet forces facing the German bulge at Orel, from where the northern pincer against Kursk had been launched, started their counter-offensive. Moving from the northern side of the bulge, Red Army units advanced south-east in an attempt to envelop the German forces before they could withdraw to the west. 2. Panzerarmee reacted swiftly and switched three Panzer Divisions (9, 20 and 18) north to meet the Soviet thrust aimed at Orel,

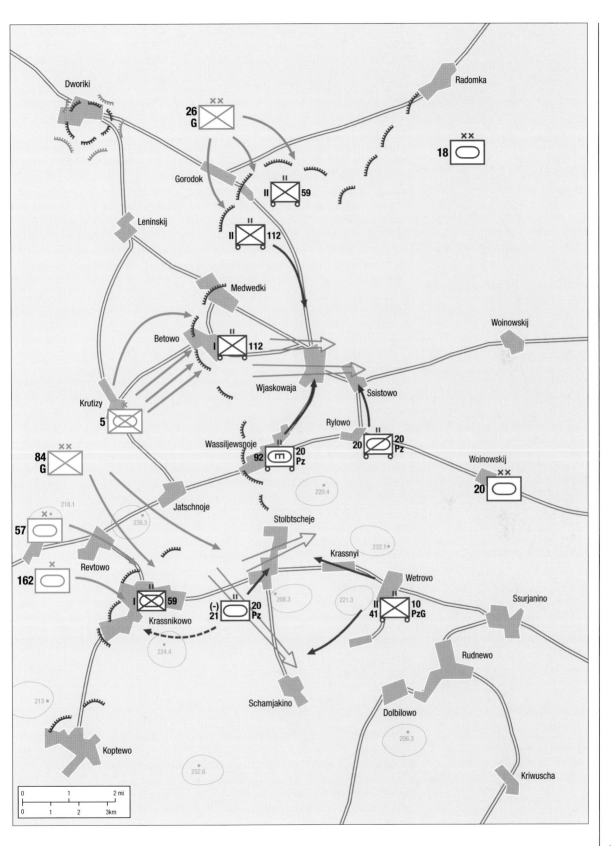

Defence at Orel, 16 July 1943.

which was to face an unexpected hurdle: the heavy rains that fell during the month. On 16 July the Soviet 26th Guards Division advanced south and attacked the positions held by 18. Panzer Division, which gathered under its command 20. Panzer Division's II./PzGrenRgt 59 (Kampfgruppe Hitzerodt) and II./PzGrenRgt 112, both defending the village of Gorodok. The Soviet attack, supported by heavy artillery, stormed the German positions, which succeeded in driving it back. To help the defenders of Godorok and to try to rescue the rear area elements of 18. Panzer Division, which had been surrounded at Dworiki, Panzer Abteilung 21 (20. Panzer Division's only tank unit) was brought forward and started moving north. Soon it ran into the 84th Guards Division's leading elements that had broken through the German defences between Krassnikowo and Wassiljewsnoje. What followed was a brief but ferocious clash during which the German Panzers managed to destroy four enemy tanks and to kill a large number of Red Army soldiers. However, at about 1:00 p.m. Panzer Abteilung 21 was forced to pull back to Krassnikowo in order to refuel and reload with ammunition. II./Panzergrenadier Regiment 41 (from 10. Infanterie Division) was sent to deal with the Soviet breakthroughs, which it halted at Schamjakino and Krassnyj. The German situation worsened when two Soviet tank brigades, plus elements from the 84th Guards Division, attacked the German stronghold at Krassnikowo held by I./PzGrenRgt 59, while to the north the Soviet 5th Armoured Brigade attacked the stronghold at Betowo held by I./PzGrenRgt 112. Fighting tenaciously, and with the support of the tanks of Panzer Abteilung 21, I./PzGrenRgt 59 held its stronghold, though it soon became clear that the threat was not yet over. At Betowo the crisis fully developed when Soviet armour broke through the stronghold of I./PzGrenRgt 112 and advanced to Wjaskowaja and Ssistowo. They were dealt with by Panzer Aufklärungs Abteilung 20, which counter-attacked in the afternoon with support from both the Panzer Pionier Bataillon 92 from the south and elements of II./PzGrenRgt 112 from the north. The Soviet drive was temporarily halted, but it was now clear to the Germans that this was a battle that could not be won. The German stronghold tactics, closely resembling those that the French had used in June 1940 during the second part of the campaign, could only work if reserves were available to counter-attack promptly and to restore the line. It had worked at Belyj eight months before, but now the Germans were fighting a 'robbing Peter to pay Paul' battle, in which units holding the strongholds also had to counter-attack the enemy breakthroughs. The Germans succeeded in inflicting heavy losses on the attacking forces, but the Red Army absorbed them and kept up its attacks, while the Germans were no longer able to cope with their own losses. The following day, both 20 and 18. Panzer Divisions began to pull back slowly in order to gain time and to allow 4. Panzerarmee's units to move west, away from the threat of encirclement. Less than a fortnight later, on 1 February, the order came to withdraw to the defence line to the west of the Orel bulge. It was the first of many such retreats.

An armoured Schützen unit mounted on Schützen Panzerwagen (armoured infantry carriers) prepares to attack enemy positions during the winter of 1941/42. Amidst the SdKfz 251 armoured personnel carriers is an SdKfz 223 leichte Funk Panzerspähwagen (light radio armoured car), detached from the divisional Nachrichten Abteilung to maintain communication.

Weapons and equipment

The Panzer Divisions reached their peak fighting strength in June 1941, although their paper strength actually peaked in December 1942 at 27 Panzer Divisions. Never again would the Panzerwaffe be able to deploy its spearhead units to such a high level of combat readiness – the result of a mixture of available personnel (both well trained and experienced), weapons, vehicles, equipment and tanks. Limited availability and the growing personnel shortage would only occasionally produce a few combat-worthy Panzer Divisions. However, the Panzer Divisions were not in a state of full readiness in June 1941; on the contrary, several shortages were still evident.

Only three out of the 19 Panzer Divisions either deployed for *Barbarossa* or held in reserve (2 and 5. Panzer Divisions) had three Abteilungen equipped with German tanks in their Panzer Regiments (3, 17 and 18. Panzer Divisions); ten others were equipped with German tanks as well, though only two had Panzer Abteilungen. Six other Panzer Divisions still had their Panzer Regiment equipped with Czech tanks, even if they all had three Panzer Abteilungen. The situation was not much better for the Schützen; only six divisions had a self-propelled schwere Infanteriegeschütz Kompanie attached to their brigade, and only 1. Panzer Division fielded one Schützen Panzerwagen-equipped battalion in each of its two Schützen Regiments. 10. Panzer Division fielded a single SPW-mounted battalion and all other divisions, but three that had no SPW at

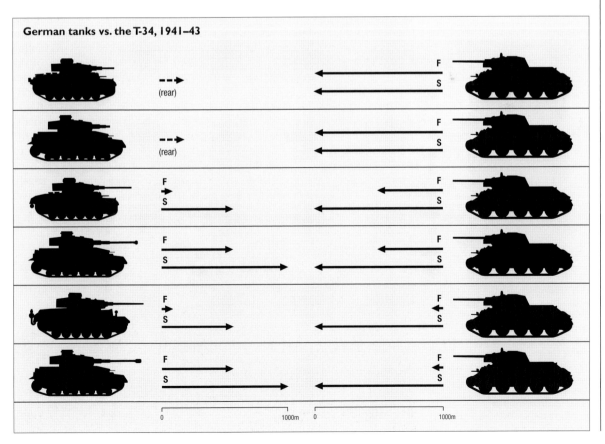

German tanks vs. the T-34, 1941–43

Table 5: Panzer Division tank strength, June 1942–November 1942 (Operational tanks in the Panzer Regiment)

Div	Date		Pz II		Pz III / Pz 38 t		Pz IV		PzBefh
1. PzDiv	15 July =	(28)	2 Pz II	(36)	10 Pz 38 t / 26 Pz III K	(14)	7 Pz IV K	(4)	4 PzBefh
	18 Nov =		3 Pz II		7 Pz 38 t / 16 + 8 + 6 Pz III		5 + 6 Pz IV		4 PzBefh
2. PzDiv	20 June =	(28)	22 Pz II	(36)	33 Pz 38 t / 20 Pz III K	(14)	5 Pz IV K	(4)	2 PzBefh
	18 Nov =		11 Pz II		10 + 8 + 12 Pz III		4 + 8 Pz IV		1 PzBefh
3. PzDiv	27 June =	(74)	25 Pz II	(106)	66 + 40 Pz III	(42)	21 + 12 Pz IV	(8)	
	18 Nov =		13 Pz II		19 + 25 Pz III		5 + 3 Pz IV		
4. PzDiv	1 July =	(33)	13 Pz II	(53)	28 Pz III K	(14)	5 Pz IV K	(4)	2 PzBefh
	18 Nov =		2 Pz II		12 Pz III K		5 Pz IV K		
5. PzDiv	25 June =	(61)	26 Pz II	(105)	55 Pz III K	(28)	13 Pz IV K	(8)	9 PzBefh
	18 Nov =		15 Pz II		23 + 10 + 7 Pz III		10 + 6 Pz IV		7 PzBefh
8. PzDiv	28 June =	(51)	1 Pz II	(71)	65 Pz 38 t	(28)	2 Pz IV K	(6)	
	18 Nov =				14 Pz 38 t				1 PzBefh
9. PzDiv	22 June =	(74)	22 Pz II	(106)	38 + 61 Pz III	(42)	9 + 12 Pz IV	(8)	2 PzBefh
	18 Nov =		26 Pz II		30 + 32 Pz III		7 + 5 Pz IV		2 PzBefh
11. PzDiv (*)	25 June =	(74)	5 Pz II	(106)	14 + 110 Pz III	(42)	1 + 12 Pz IV	(8)	3 PzBefh
	18 Nov =		11 (3) Pz II		9 (2) + 49 (28) Pz III		6 (3) Pz IV L		3 (1) PzBefh
12. PzDiv	1 July =	(51)		(71)	48 Pz III K	(28)	6 + 4 Pz IV	(6)	
	18 Nov =		1 Pz II		24 + 17 Pz III		2 + 18 Pz IV		3 PzBefh
13. PzDiv	22 June =	(74)	15 Pz II	(106)	41 + 30 Pz III	(42)	12 Pz IV K	(8)	5 PzBefh
	18 Nov =		4 Pz II		7 + 14 Pz III		1 + 3 Pz IV		
14. PzDiv	20 June =	(74)	14 Pz II	(106)	41 + 19 Pz III	(42)	20 + 4 Pz IV	(8)	4 PzBefh
	18 Nov =				1 + 21 + 7 Pz III		1 + 6 Pz IV		5 PzBefh
16. PzDiv	1 July =	(74)	13 Pz II	(106)	39 + 18 Pz III	(42)	15 + 12 Pz IV	(8)	3 PzBefh
	18 Nov =				21 Pz III L		1 + 9 Pz IV		
17. PzDiv	15 July =	(28)	17 Pz II	(36)	36 Pz III K	(14)	16 Pz IV K	(4)	2 PzBefh
	18 Nov =		9 Pz II		30 Pz III K		18 Pz IV K		3 PzBefh
18. PzDiv	15 July =	(28)	11 Pz II	(36)	26 Pz III K	(14)	8 Pz IV K	(2)	2 PzBefh
	18 Nov =		5 Pz II		22 + 0 + 6 Pz III		4 + 9 Pz IV		2 PzBefh
19. PzDiv	15 July =	(33)	6 Pz II	(53)	35 Pz 38 t/12 Pz III K	(14)	4 Pz IV K	(4)	
	18 Nov =		7 Pz II		37 Pz 38 t/8 Pz III K		3 + 10 Pz IV		3 PzBefh
20. PzDiv	30 June =	(28)	8 Pz II	(36)	39 Pz 38 t /20 Pz III K	(14)	13 Pz IV K	(4)	7 PzBefh
	18 Nov =		4 Pz II		22 Pz 38 t /14 Pz III K		11 + 5 Pz IV		6 PzBefh
22. PzDiv	1 July =	(51)	28 Pz II	(71)	114 Pz 38 t /12 Pz III L	(28)	11 + 11 Pz IV	(6)	
	18 Nov =		2 Pz II		5 Pz 38 t/0 + 12 + 10 Pz III		1 + 10 Pz IV		
23. PzDiv	28 June =	(74)	27 Pz II	(106)	50 + 34 Pz III	(42)	17 + 10 Pz IV	(8)	
	18 Nov =		5 Pz II		12 + 15 Pz III		4 + 4 Pz IV		
24. PzDiv	28 June =	(74)	32 Pz II	(106)	54 + 56 Pz III	(42)	20 + 12 Pz IV	(8)	7 PzBefh
	18 Nov =		5 Pz II		9 + 17 + 5 Pz III		5 + 12 Pz IV		2 PzBefh
27. PzDiv	18 Nov =		9 Pz II		22 Pz 38 t / 5 + 10 + 12 Pz III		2 + 5 Pz IV		
6. PzDiv	late Nov =	[21]	21 Pz II	[105]	0 + 73 + 32 Pz III	[20]	24 Pz IV L	[6]	9 PzBefh
7. PzDiv	January 43	[21]	21 Pz II	[105]	0 + 91 + 14 Pz III	[20]	2 + 18 Pz IV	[6]	9 PzBefh

(*) I./PzRgt 15, detached to HGr Mitte.

Established strength for 22. Panzer Division does not include III./PzRgt 204; those for 6 and 7. PzDiv are given according to actual figures in late 1942.

Figures in brackets and bold are the established strength; this is followed by actual tank strength. For the PzKpfw III the first figure (if any) shows the 37mm gun-armed tanks, the second shows the 50mm gun L/42 (also shown by the letter K close to a single figure) and the third one the 50mm L/60 gun-armed tanks (also marked with the letter L). For the PzKpfw IV the first figure shows the short-barrelled 75mm gun (also shown by the letter K), the second the 75mm long-barrelled gun-armed tanks (also shown by the letter L with a single figure).

all were equipped only with a single Kompanie. Moreover, 20. Panzer Division had been fully motorized by the use of captured French vehicles, which were technically inferior to the German ones. Similarly, due to the limited production of armoured cars, its Panzer Aufklärungs Abteilung and that of 7. Panzer Division were equipped with captured French armoured cars, though both had two rather than the customary single Panzer Späh Kompanie.

The artillery was in much better shape. All the divisions had six 105mm leichte Feldhaubitze 18 batteries and three 150mm schwere Feldhaubitze 18 towed batteries; only six of them replaced one of the latter with a 105mm Kanone 18 battery. Inadequate production again hampered the re-equipment of the Panzerjäger Abteilung with the new 50mm anti-tank gun PAK 38. Since this was the newest and most effective anti-tank weapon in the German inventory, priority was given to those Panzer Divisions equipped with the Czech tanks and those that had three companies each with only four of the obsolete 37mm PAK 35/36 and six of the new PAK 38. However, 12. Panzer Division had only eight 37mm and three 47mm Czech anti-tank guns in each PAK Kompanie, while two other Panzer Divisions (19 and 20) had no Fla Kompanie. All other Panzer Divisions were still equipped with eight PAK 35/36 and only three PAK 38 in each of their PAK Kompanien, and 3. Panzer Division (whose Panzerjäger Abteilung had been used to create 5. leichte Division for North Africa) had only three PAK Kompanien equipped with 12 ageing 37mm PAK 35/36. However, all the Panzer Pionier Bataillone had been equipped with their full complement of PzKpfw I and with rocket launcher-equipped SdKfz 251 half-tracks. Also, all the divisions had a full establishment of motor vehicles in their supply and support units (see tables 1 to 3 on pp. 12–18).

Quite clearly the attempts made to achieve uniform organization among the available Panzer Divisions had been unsuccessful, and that had inevitable consequences at a later stage. Yet there is no evidence to suggest that such differences actually influenced their performance in the field, at least during *Barbarossa* and up to December 1941. What actually influenced performance were both attrition and the widespread lack of replacements, which were to affect the fighting power and the combat effectiveness of the Panzer Divisions as early as summer 1941. The best example, and also the most interesting one, is the German tank situation on the Eastern Front and how it evolved during *Barbarossa* and the months to follow. On 1 June 1941 the German tank inventory included a total of 5,262 tanks, of which 4,198 were considered suitable for combat, plus 377 Sturmgeschütz. In comparison with the situation on 1 September 1939 (a total of 3,263 tanks, of which 2,690 were operational) and on 10 May 1940 (a total of 3,505 tanks, of which about 2,580 were operational), the figures had not really improved, since one must consider not only that in June 1941 the Panzerwaffe fielded twice the number of Panzer Divisions as in May 1940 but also that it was now engaged on two fronts – against the Soviet Union and in North Africa. However, the quality had improved; the breakdown includes 1,072 PzKpfw II (plus 85 flame-throwers), 754 PzKpfw 38 (t), 1,440 PzKpfw III armed with either the 37mm or the 50mm L 24 gun, 517 PzKpfw IV and 330 Panzer Befehlswagen, to which must be added 877 PzKpfw I and 187 PzKpfw 35 (t), which though considered unsuitable for the front, were still in use. This means there were more than three times the number of PzKpfw III available in May 1940 (429), though less than twice the number of PzKpfw IV (296) and about twice the number of PzKpfw 38 (t) available. Shortages of PzKpfw IV tanks eventually led to the number of PzKpfw IV Zug (platoons) in the mittlere Panzer Kompanie falling

A Panzer Division Kampfgruppe readies itself to move during the Operation *Zitadelle* offensive against the Kursk salient, July 1943. The basic camouflage colour of German vehicles was changed from *Panzergrau* to dark yellow–green–brown only on 18 February 1943. The new scheme can be seen on the PzKpfw IV Ausf G on the left. Though the order required other vehicles to be repainted in this fashion, the pressure on time and resources meant that in most cases only mud was applied over the original grey.

from three to two, a relatively common occurrence that was never quite rectified until 1943.

Of course, only a limited number of the available tanks had been deployed on the Eastern Front by June 1941. The overall strength was 3,377 tanks, their bulk (3,152) being in the Panzer Divisions (figures greatly vary according to different sources; these and the following figures are the most uniform). The breakdown indicates 162 PzKpfw I (133 in the Panzer Division), 774 PzKpfw II (706), 84 Panzer Flammwagen II, 286 PzKpfw III armed with the 37mm gun (276), 648 PzKpfw III armed with the 50mm gun (648), 155 PzKpfw 35 (t) (all in 6. Panzer Division), 625 PzKpfw 38 (t) (all in 7, 8, 12, 19 and 20. Panzer Divisions), 426 PzKpfw IV (423) and 198 PzBefh (186). As is shown in Table 3 on page 18, in June 1941 the Panzer Regiment had already suffered from a shortage of both the 'light' PzKpfw II and the 'heavy' PzKpfw IV, while in the meantime, 'medium' tanks such as the PzKpfw III and the Czech tanks were at full strength. In contrast, by June 1941 the Red Army had 1,861 modern tanks, such as the T-34s and the KVs, out of a total of 22,600 (of which 14,200 were with the field forces) tanks and self-propelled guns, most of which were old and obsolete. Yet it is also clear that the Panzerwaffe took the upper hand with its enemy from the very outset and held it until the last year of war. Up until September or October 1941 the Red Army had lost some 15,000 tanks, a figure that rose to about 20,500 by the end of the year and which is more than 90 per cent of the initial field strength, or 75 per cent of the total availability, which included 4,700 tanks produced during the year. Compared with German tank losses, these figures appear even more staggering. Until September 1941 the Germans lost a total of 1,734 tanks (358 PzKpfw I, 259 PzKpfw II all types, 354 PzKpfw III, 460 PzKpfw 38, 41 PzKpfw 35, 215 PzKpfw IV and 47 PzBefh), a figure that rose to more than 3,252 at the end of December 1942 (450 PzKpfw I, 492 PzKpfw II, 820 PzKpfw III, 823 PzKpfw 38, 396 PzKpfw IV and 116 PzBefh; apparently 6. Panzer Division lost all of its tanks, bringing the grand total to 3,252). Though markedly inferior to the Soviet numbers, these figures are remarkably close to the total number of tanks fielded at the beginning of *Barbarossa*, which means that, with its limited production and even more limited allocation, it was the Panzerwaffe that suffered most.

Three factors affected the armoured component of the Panzerwaffe during the first stage of war on the Eastern Front; first, attrition; second, inadequate tank production and replacement; and, third, the technical superiority of the Soviet tanks. Attrition took its toll as early as the first months of war, though apparently tank losses were not due only to enemy action but rather, to a greater or lesser extent, to mechanical breakdown. By 9 July 1941, Panzer Regiment 6 of 3. Panzer Division had permanently lost 13 of its 58 PzKpfw II, 24 of its 110 PzKpfw III and eight of its 32 PzKpfw IV; two PzKpfw II and seven PzKpfw III were in repair, and the division still had some 144 tanks fully operational. By the end of the month

A Panzer Regiment advances through a Soviet city passing a column of Schützen infantry, autumn 1941. The turret number on the PzKpfw II in the foreground, which reads '6 L 1', probably denotes the first tank of the leichte Panzer Zug of a sixth Panzer Kompanie. In the background, a PzKpfw I can be seen passing a PzKpfw III; some 150 PzKpfw I tanks were still in use by the Panzer regiments on the Eastern Front in 1941.

Table 6: Panzer Division tank strength on the Eastern Front, I July 1943

2. PzDiv	II./PzRgt 3	12 Pz II	Pz III = 8 + 12 + 20	I + 59 Pz IV	6 PzBefh
3. PzDiv	II./PzRgt 6	7 Pz II	Pz III = 8 + 34 + 17	2 + 21 Pz IV	I PzBefh
4. PzDiv	I./PzRgt 35		Pz III = 15 (75mm)	I + 79 Pz IV	6 PzBefh
5. PzDiv	II./PzRgt 31		Pz III = 17 (75mm)	76 Pz IV (L)	9 PzBefh
6. PzDiv	II./PzRgt II	13 Pz II	Pz III = 0 + 34 + 18 / 14 Fl	32 Pz IV (L)	6 PzBefh
7. PzDiv	I–II./PzRgt 25	12 Pz II	Pz III = 0 + 43 + 12	I + 37 Pz IV	7 PzBefh
8. PzDiv	I./PzRgt 10	14 Pz II	Pz 38 = 3		
			Pz III = 25 + 30 + 4	8 + 14 Pz IV	6 PzBefh
9. PzDiv	II./PzRgt 33	I Pz II	Pz III = 8 + 30	8 + 30 Pz IV	6 PzBefh
II. PzDiv	II–III./PzRgt 15	8 Pz II	Pz III = 11 + 51 / 13 Fl	I + 25 Pz IV	4 PzBefh
12. PzDiv	II./PzRgt 29	6 Pz II	Pz III = 15 + 15 + 6	I + 36 Pz IV	4 PzBefh
13. PzDiv	I–II./PzRgt 4	5 Pz II	Pz III = 4 + 10	50 Pz IV (L)	2 PzBefh
17. PzDiv	II./PzRgt 39	4 Pz II	Pz III = I + 19 + 9	I + 31 Pz IV	2 PzBefh
18. PzDiv	PzAbt 18	5 Pz II	Pz III = 10 + 0 + 20	5 + 29 Pz IV	3 PzBefh
19. PzDiv	I–II./PzRgt 27	2 Pz II	Pz III = 5 + 22 + 11	2 + 36 Pz IV	3 PzBefh
20. PzDiv	PzAbt 21		Pz 38 t = 9		
			Pz III = 2 + 10 + 5	9 + 40 Pz IV	7 PzBefh
23. PzDiv	I./PzRgt 201	I Pz II	Pz III = 7 + 17 + 3	30 Pz IV (L)	I PzBefh

Figures for the PzKpfw III show 50mm short-barrelled + 50mm long-barrelled + 75mm short-barrelled gun-armed tanks/Flammpanzer (also Fl) flame-thrower tanks. Figures for the PzKpfw IV show 75mm short-barrelled + 75mm long-barrelled (denoted by an L) gun-armed tanks.

Panzer Regiment 6 had another four PzKpfw III write-offs and had about 50 tanks under repair (three PzKpfw II, 39 PzKpfw III and eight PzKpfw IV), which along with tanks handed over to other units, brought its total strength to 35 PzKpfw II, 35 PzKpfw III and 16 PzKpfw IV. On 21 July 1941, Panzer Regiment 25 of 7. Panzer Division reported it had lost all of its 53 PzKpfw II, 112 of its 167 PzKpfw 38 (t), 15 of its 30 PzKpfw IV and eight of its 15 PzBefh. Since most of these were undergoing repair (24 PzKpfw II, 78 PzKpfw 38, 10 PzKpfw IV and five PzBefh), total write-offs were limited to 29 PzKpfw II, 34 PzKpfw 38 (t), five PzKpfw IV and three PzBefh. Clearly the Panzer Divisions were still able to fight on, in spite of the constant attrition, due to their efficient field maintenance system that enabled prompt recovery in most instances. However, in the long run this did not prevent a constant reduction in their combat effectiveness. A full recovery required either a long period of rest or adequate replacements. The Panzer Divisions received neither.

In mid-July 1941 Hitler released only 70 PzKpfw III and 15 PzKpfw IV, plus the available Czech tanks, to the Eastern Front as replacements, in spite of reports that showed how tank losses were as high as 50 per cent of the actual strength (though this figure probably included tanks in repair). The decision was made to preserve tank production for the new Panzer Divisions being raised. Thus, in spite of the gloominess of the situation, by September 1941 only 137 replacement tanks had made their way to the Eastern Front; a statistic of 5 September reported that out of a total tank strength of 3,397 only 1,586 Panzers, about 47 per cent, were still fully operational. Total losses amounted to 702 write-offs and about another 542 tanks in repair along with 557 tanks whose fate was uncertain, though estimates reported that as much as 30 per cent of total strength had been permanently lost while about 23 per cent was undergoing repair. On average, the Panzer Divisions had 34 per cent of their established tank strength. Overall, Panzergruppe 4 was in

A PzKpfw 35 (t) of 6. Panzer Division passes a farmhouse in Lithuania, June 1941. By this time it was the only division still equipped with this obsolete tank, which performed poorly in cold weather. The last one to see service, nicknamed 'Anthony the Last', broke down on 10 December 1941 near Klin, thus depriving 6. Panzer Division of proper armour.

better shape with as much as 70 per cent of its established tank strength still operational; both Panzergruppe 1 (with 53 per cent operational) and 3 (with 41 per cent) were average, while Panzergruppe 2 was left with only 25 per cent of its operational strength. Though these figures are only approximate, Table 3 on page 18 reveals how close to the truth they are. With a few exceptions, write-off tanks represented only a limited percentage of losses, though on average, the operational tanks left were about half of those available in June. This situation was also a consequence of inadequate provisions for tank repair, since those earmarked for long-term repair that could not be undertaken at field workshops had to be sent back to Germany.

A long rest or adequate replacements would have spared the Panzer Divisions from the predations of attrition, yet the only improvement was the arrival on the Eastern Front in September of the last two uncommitted Panzer Divisions, which added some 380 tanks. The already depleted tank strength would shrink even further during the attack on Moscow, until the Soviet offensive of December 1941 eventually brought about final disaster. By mid-December 2. Panzerarmee had only 40 tanks left out of the 248 that were available in mid-October; and Panzergruppe 3 had only 34 left out of the 259 available in mid-October. By January 1942 only 1,138 replacement tanks had reached the Eastern Front, or 35 per cent of the total loss suffered of 3,252 tanks in the same period, itself a figure too close for comfort to the 3,377 tanks deployed in June 1941.

The reorganization of spring 1942 introduced the two-tier concept that saw some divisions being brought up to strength to take part in the new offensive, while other divisions were left untouched, if not further depleted by detachments. As a result, only a few Panzer Divisions recovered some kind of full effectiveness, while most were only partially operational and some others were unable to take part in offensive operations. A report by the Heeresgruppe Süd (Army Group South) of 30 April 1942 bore this out: 'Owing to diverse composition, partial lack of battle experience and gaps in their outfitting, the units available for the summer operation in 1942 will not have the combat effectiveness that could be taken for granted at the beginning of the campaign in the East. The mobile units, too, will not have the flexibility, the endurance, or the penetrating power they had a year ago.'[2]

Tank production is partly to blame for this state of affairs. Since the victory in France in June 1940, tank production had seen a steady increase, though it never reached peak levels, and only in October were 211 tanks and assault guns of all types produced. This production level was again reached in January 1941, though only because the following May production reached an average of 300 per month, increasing to 370 in August. The figure rose in November 1941 to 399, before rising again to 433 in February 1942, only to decrease to 336 the next month. In the second half of 1940 production focused on the main battle tanks and only some 70 PzKpfw II were rebuilt for use as flame-throwers; in the same period a total of 604 PzKpfw III were produced, 138 with the 37mm gun and 466 with the 50mm L/42 gun. Comparing these figures with production between September 1939 and May 1940 (432 examples built) shows how limited the increase had been. Also, in the second half of 1940, 245 PzKpfw 38 (t), 186 PzKpfw IV and 29 PzBefh were produced. Between January and June 1941 the figures again saw a slight increase: 49 PzKpfw II (production was restarted in February), 688 PzKpfw III (all with the 50mm gun), 340 PzKpfw 38 (t), 188 PzKpfw IV and 101 PzBefh were built. The beginning of *Barbarossa* brought

2 Quoted in: Earl F. Ziemke and Magna E. Bauer, *Moscow to Stalingrad*, page 328.

another increase, and, in the second half of 1941, 184 PzKpfw II, 1,025 PzKpfw III (including 64 armed with the 50mm L/60 gun), 358 PzKpfw 38 (t), 292 PzKpfw IV and 31 PzBefh were produced. However, a comparison with the total losses suffered in the second half of 1941 reveals a grim reality: 393 PzKpfw II (against 233 produced), 782 PzKpfw III (against 2,317 produced), 773 PzKpfw 38 (t) (against 943 produced), 369 PzKpfw IV (against 666 produced) and 96 PzBefh (against 161 produced).

Quite clearly, the PzKpfw III was now the main German battle tank. Yet the PzKpfw III was no longer a tank capable of dealing with enemy tanks on equal terms. Since the beginning of *Barbarossa*, the Panzer Divisions suffered not only from the consequences of their numerical but also their technical inferiority when compared with the heavy Soviet tanks such as the KVs and T-34s. A stopgap measure was the improvement of anti-tank guns and self-propelled vehicles, though the Panzer remained the main weapon. Improvements were, once more, belated; in spite of the increased needs, production in the first half of 1942 saw only 256 PzKpfw II, 1,339 PzKpfw III (of which 1,042 were armed with the 50mm L/60 gun), 195 PzKpfw 38 (t) (production ceased in June), 362 PzKpfw IV (of which 237 were armed with the 75mm L/43 gun) and 14 PzBefh built. By 1 June 1942 the German tank inventory included 979 PzKpfw II (deemed non-battle-worthy but still in high demand for their role in reconnaissance); 454 PzKpfw 38 (t) (non-battle-worthy, though hard to replace); 2,306 PzKpfw III; 681 PzKpfw IV; and 264 PzBefh. As opposed to the figures of the year before, these reveal how overall tank strength increased (5,385 versus 5,262 in 1941), though the German Army still largely depended on obsolete and non-battle-worthy tanks since the battle-worthy ones only numbered 3,251 against the 4,198 of June 1941.

By 1 July 1942 total tank strength on the Eastern Front was 2,535, which is one-quarter fewer than it had been in the previous June. Table 5 on page 64 shows how, in June and July 1942, the Panzer Divisions dramatically suffered from shortages of PzKpfw II and how they still heavily relied on the PzKpfw 38 (t) and the short-barrelled PzKpfw III and IV. Between late June and mid-July, overall tank strength in the Panzer Divisions included 297 PzKpfw II, 614 short-barrelled PzKpfw III, 380 long-barrelled PzKpfw III, 296 PzKpfw 38 (t), 205 short-barrelled PzKpfw IV, 89 long-barrelled PzKpfw IV and 52 PzBefh. With about 2,000 tanks, the Panzer Divisions were still the main spearhead of the German Army in the East.

Production of the PzKpfw II ceased in July 1942 with the last 20 examples built, and given the lack of any suitable replacement, this was a tank that the Panzer Divisions would miss in the months to come. However, tank production was now fully steered to meet the demands of the battlefield. In the second half of 1942, 1,266 PzKpfw III were produced, now armed only with the 50mm L/60 gun (production ceased in December) or with the 75mm L/24 equipping the PzKpfw IV (449 produced in 1942). Production of the PzKpfw IV now stood at

A column of PzKpfw 38 (t) tanks moves along a muddy road in autumn 1941. At the beginning of *Barbarossa* there were still 625 such tanks equipping the regiments of the 7, 8, 12, 19 and 20. Panzer divisions. By June 1942 this number had fallen to 318, even though production had ceased in December 1941. The use of the 38 (t) chassis for the Marder III self-propelled anti-tank gun soon led to this tank's disappearance from service.

Table 7 – Comparison of the Panzer III and IV and the T-34, 1941–43

	Weight (tons)	Speed (km/h)	Main armament	Armour (mm)		
				front	side	rear
PzKpfw III Ausf H / J [1]	21.5	42	50mm KwK L/42	30–50	30	30–50
PzKpfw III Ausf L / M	22.7	40	50mm KwK 39 L/60	50–57	30	30–50
PzKpfw IV Ausf E	21	42	75mm KwK 37 L/24	30–50	20	20
PzKpfw IV Ausf F	22.3	42	75mm KwK 37 L/24	50	30	20–30
PzKpfw IV Ausf F 2 [2]	23	40	75mm KwK 40 L/43	50	30	20–30
PzKPfw IV Ausf G	23.5	38	75mm KwK 40 L/48	50	30	20–30
T-34 Model 1940	28.5	55	76.2mm L/30	45	45	40
T-34 Model 1943	30.9	53	76.2mm F 34	60–70	45–52	45–52

Armour does not include appliqué armour; it indicates the main armour on the hull and turret.
The speed given is the maximum on-road.
[1] *The PzKpfw III Ausf J was retrofitted with the 50mm KwK 39 L/60 gun.*
[2] *The PzKpfw IV Ausf G had a 30mm appliqué armour plate on the hull front.*

632, all armed with the L/43 gun (36 PzBefh were also produced). Tank strength on the Eastern Front on 18 November 1942 shows how the situation had changed since *Barbarossa*; in total there were 164 PzKpfw II (135 with the Panzer Divisions), 107 PzKpfw 38 (t) (all with the Panzer Divisions), 264 short-barrelled 50mm gun PzKpfw III (261 with the Panzer Divisions), 381 long-barrelled 50mm gun PzKpfw III (287 with the Panzer Division), 93 PzKpfw III with the 75mm gun (65 with the Panzer Divisions), 99 short-barrelled 75mm PzKpfw IV (91 with the Panzer Divisions), 183 long- barrelled 75mm gun PzKpfw IV (128 with the Panzer Divisions) and 50 PzBefh (43 with the Panzer Divisions). The sharp difference between production and actual strength was explained partly by losses, which included in 1942 some 287 PzKpfw II, 1,501 PzKpfw III (against 2,605 produced), 196 PzKpfw 38 (t), 502 PzKpfw IV (against 994 produced) and 99 PzBefh. The increased number of Panzer Divisions and the demands from the other fronts added further strain to the Panzerwaffe.

It is worth noting that, in spite of their deficiencies, the Germans still held the upper hand against Red Army armour. On 1 January 1942 the Soviets had 7,700 tanks and self-propelled guns, 2,200 of which were with the field forces; another 24,500 were produced during the year. Yet the Germans destroyed some 15,100 of them during the year, nearly 47 per cent of the entire availability – although it is hard to say how many can be credited to the Panzer Divisions (and also which weapon actually destroyed them). When the Germans first met the Soviet KV and T-34 tanks in June 1941 they were stunned, though they had already experienced fighting against enemy tanks with heavy armour. However, given its speed, mobility, invulnerability and powerful gun, it was the T-34 that most impressed the Germans. It did not take long before the German tankers began referring to the T-34 as a 'war-winning weapon', which it could have been had it not suffered from the same shortcomings that affected the French tanks in 1940 (a lack of radio equipment, available only in command tanks, and a two-man turret that interfered with the tank commander's main role) and, above all, if their crews had not suffered from a lack of training and experience. Additionally, in the early stages of *Barbarossa* the T-34s were used in small groups, pairs or at most five tanks, which the Germans could deal with. Bigger problems arose in autumn 1941 when the Soviets began using their tanks en masse, which was very hard to defend against.

The German tanks in 1941 were easy prey to the T-34s, which could only be disabled if the Panzer placed a hit close to the rear sprocket wheel at a very close range, between 100m and 200m. The T-34s could easily hit (both on the sides and front) and destroy the German tanks at 1,000m or more. Since even the 50mm PAK 38 was all but useless against the T-34s and the KVs, the only readily available solution was a stopgap one: to use captured Soviet 76.2mm anti-tank guns, preferably mounted on the chassis of otherwise obsolete tanks. The first self-propelled Panzerjäger were produced from April 1942, either on the PzKpfw II chassis (Marder II, from June 1942, also armed with a 75mm PAK 40 gun) or on that of the PzKpfw 38 (t) (Marder III, from November 1942, also armed with a 75mm PAK 40 gun). In 1942, 184 Marder II with the 76.2mm gun and 327 Marder II with the 75mm gun (figures for 1943 are respectively eight and 204) were built, plus 344 Marder III with the 76.2mm gun and another 110 with the 75mm gun (in 1943, 19 and 799 examples were produced). Production of the already obsolete 37mm PAK 35/36 was finally halted in 1941 (though 32 more were produced in 1942), while production of the 50mm PAK 38 rose from 388 in 1940 to 2,072 in 1941 and eventually to 4,480 in 1942 (in 1943 only 2,626 examples were produced). The 75mm PAK 97/38, a captured French gun, was introduced into service in large quantities to fight against the Soviet T-34 and KV tanks (2,854 in 1942), but it was only with the new 75mm PAK 40 that the Germans acquired a suitable anti-tank weapon (2,114 produced in 1942, 8,740 in 1943). From 1942, the Panzer Divisions' Panzerjäger Abteilungen were made up of a mixture of towed and self-propelled anti-tank guns, ranging from the 37mm PAK 35/36 to the newest 75mm PAK 40, and only ten divisions had a self-propelled anti-tank gun company. Yet, anti-tank guns were a defensive weapon and, to maintain some offensive capabilities, improvements were badly needed for the tanks.

With the *Lang* (long-barrelled) 50mm and 75mm guns mounted on the PzKpfw III and IV in 1942, it was possible to restore some kind of offensive power to the Panzers. Although the former was only effective against the T-34 at very short range if firing frontally (100m), it was otherwise effective at c. 500m when firing against the sides, the same range at which the long-barrelled PzKpfw IV could effectively engage the T-34 frontally. Also, long-barrelled PzKpfw IV were able to engage the side of a T-34 at about 1,000m. Matching these performances with the improved armour on the German tanks, which reduced to 500m the distance at which a T-34 could effectively engage them frontally, it is clear that some kind of offensive power had been restored. However, the peak had been reached and, until the Panther tank became available to the Panzer Divisions (which happened in September 1943), their main battle tanks could improve their armour but not their guns. In fact, the new models of PzKpfw III and IV introduced in 1943 maintained their guns unaltered but, thanks to increased armour, now reduced to about 100m the effective range at which the T-34 could challenge them frontally. This was not done without cost, since the reduced speed, mobility and manoeuvrability of the German tanks also affected speed, mobility and the manoeuvre capabilities of the Panzer units. This also was a step toward the shift from firepower to mobility, as German tank production figures in the first half of 1943 show: these included 215 PzKpfw III (production was halted in August with the last 20 examples) against 1,277 PzKpfw IV, which now became the Panzer Divisions' main battle tank – the first 324 Panthers were delivered only in May 1943 and were used to form independent brigades.

A PzKpfw III Ausf L in a queue of traffic along a congested road awaits the completion of a bridge, summer 1942. The first version of the PzKpfw III to mount the 50mm KwK 39 L/60 was the Ausf J, produced from December 1941; the Ausf L entered production in June 1942, but it was soon used to mount the 75mm L/24 gun, becoming the Ausf N. A total of 653 examples of the Ausf L were built before production ceased in December 1942.

A leichte Panzer Kompanie of Panzer Regiment 36, 14. Panzer Division moves through a Soviet village, summer 1942. A PzKpfw III Ausf G is in the foreground. The Panzer Divisions' involvement in the battle for Stalingrad saw them used as the army's 'battering rams', leading to the loss of three divisions in the eventual collapse of the pocket.

By July 1943 most of the Panzer Divisions had only a single Panzer Abteilung left and were still equipped with a mixture of old and new tank models. Most importantly, looking at the actual tank strength on the Eastern Front on 1 July, one can see not only that with 3,524 tanks and assault guns this was the highest figure since the beginning of *Barbarossa*, which shows how the Germans had been able to recover even from the Stalingrad disaster, but also a closer look at the total number of tanks in the Panzer Divisions (1,451) reveals how by then they were no longer the main and only instrument of warfare available to the German Army. Rather, they had now become just one of the many instruments of warfare that included, amongst others, the Panzergrenadier Division, both Army and Waffen-SS, plus the independent tanks and assault gun units (the three Waffen-SS Panzergrenadier Divisions had a total tank strength of 494; 90 Tiger tanks were in two independent schwere Panzer Abteilungen and 305 assault guns were in the independent Sturmgeschütz Abteilungen). Along with such fragmentation, there is another factor to take into account. As the breakdown of the Panzer Divisions' tank strength reveals, in spite of the still heavily mixed composition, the trend was now unmistakable. In fact, those 1,451 tanks included 90 PzKpfw II, 611 PzKpfw III (all types), 12 PzKpfw 38 (t), 665 PzKpfw IV (short- and long-barrelled) and 73 PzBefh. There could no longer be any doubt; the age of the light, fast-moving tanks was coming to an end, and the age of the heavily armoured and strongly armed tanks had begun.

The changes did not affect the Panzer units alone, though in most cases they occurred only to a limited extent to the other units of the Panzer Divisions. The exception was the use of armoured personnel carriers, and not only by the Schützen units. Limited production of the main Schützen Panzerwagen, the SdKfz 251, prevented the Schützen units from becoming true armoured infantry. The same applied to the new, light Schützen Panzerwagen, the SdKfz 250, which was put into service in June 1941. In this case too, limited production prevented its widespread use. Both the SdKfz 251 and the 250 were used in many roles other than just as armoured personnel carriers. These included service as command and communication vehicles, heavy weapons carriers and special engineer vehicles. Therefore, they could be, and were, used not only by the Schützen units but also by the divisional Pionier and Nachrichten units, not to mention the SdKfz 253 artillery observation vehicle used by the artillery. Given the limited production (337 SdKfz 251 were produced in 1940, 424 in 1941; 389 SdKfz 250 were produced in 1941 plus a further 285 SdKfz 253 and 414 SdKfz 252, the latter an ammunition carrier), it is not surprising that in 1941 there were only three SPW-mounted Schützen Bataillone and 14 Kompanien. In 1942 production of both vehicles increased sharply. With some 1,337 SdKfz 250 and 1,200 SdKfz 251 produced that year, it became possible not only to increase the number of SPW-mounted Schützen units (see Table 4 on page 26, which shows how the SPW became more common), but it was also possible to address another problem: the reorganization of the Kradschützen Bataillon and the lack of Panzerspähwagen, the armoured cars.

In 1941 both the Kradschützen Bataillon and the Panzer Aufklärungs Abteilung were equipped with motorcycles and light motor vehicles, the latter being also equipped with both light (four-wheeled) and heavy (eight-wheeled) armoured cars in the Panzer Späh Kompanie, the armoured car company. Problems still arose in autumn 1941 as motorized units, particularly motorcycle units, were not well suited to the poor road network of the Soviet Union, and the two reconnaissance units became all but redundant for the Panzer Divisions. At first the two were merged together as Kradschützen Bataillone and, from 1943, as the new Panzer Aufklärungs Abteilung. They were equipped partly with the SdKfz 250, which proved particularly suitable as a reconnaissance vehicle and personnel carrier. However, the shortage of armoured cars soon began to affect the reconnaissance units too. In 1940 and 1941 the production of armoured cars had been scant: only 138 (in 1940) and 290 (in 1941) light SdKfz 221, 222 and 223 were produced, along with eight (91 in 1941) light radio SdKfz 260 and 261 armoured cars, plus 26 (94 in 1941) heavy SdKfz 231 and 232 armoured cars. In 1941 other models entered production, including 54 SdKfz 247 light command armoured cars and eight SdKfz 263 heavy radio armoured cars, also used by the divisional Nachrichten Abteilung. Production was sharply increased in 1942 (414 light SdKfz 221, 222 and 223; 236 light SdKfz 260 and 261; four light SdKfz 247; 160 heavy SdKfz 231 and 232; 118 heavy SdKfz 263 and 22 heavy SdKfz 233 armed with a 75mm gun), yet this was still inadequate to meet demand. In 1943 the production of the heavy armoured cars was brought to a halt; during the year 200 SdKfz 231 and 232 were produced along with 40 SdKfz 263 and 100 SdKfz 233, and these were intended to be replaced by the new SdKfz 234 series. Production of the light armoured cars continued, though on a smaller scale; only 306 SdKfz 221, 222 and 223 were produced along with 76 SdKfz 260 and 261. By 1942 it was not possible to equip the Panzer Späh Kompanie of three Panzer Divisions (8, 18 and 20), and in January 1943 a decision was made to create the new armoured cars companies mounted on the SPW.

The old Panzer Späh Kompanie was retained and a new Geschütz Zug, equipped with the SdKfz 233, was added. But a new SPW-mounted Panzer Späh Kompanie c was also formed and equipped with 25 SdKfz 250 of various kinds. Although by July 1943 there were only ten of these, the innovation marked the definitive transition to a widespread use of the armoured personnel carriers in a variety of roles. By July 1943 ten SPW-mounted Panzergrenadier Bataillone (as they were known from July 1942) had been formed within the Panzer Divisions. Another three were formed with the divisions rebuilt after Stalingrad; also, all other Panzer Divisions had at least an SPW-mounted Panzergrenadier Kompanie (see Table 4 on page 26). That was made possible by the dramatic increase in the production of SPW in 1943; during the year some 2,895 SdKfz 250 and some 4,258 SdKfz 251 were produced, ensuring that all the Stab (HQs) of the Panzer Divisions' Panzer Pionier Bataillone along with some 19 Panzer Pionier Kompanien and all the Panzer Nachrichten Abteilungen could be re-equipped with them.

From early 1943 the Panzer Divisions began to acquire mobility and firepower on a scale without precedent, also due in part to other new

A brand new PzKpfw IV Ausf G is driven away from a depot in the rear by its crew, winter 1942. Armed with the 75mm KwK 40 L/48 gun, it was the most powerful tank in the Panzer Divisions' inventory until the Panther became available in September 1943.

weapons and vehicles. The most interesting innovation was the introduction of the self-propelled artillery guns, which gave the Panzer Divisions' artillery elements better mobility (which was much needed, since the towed heavy guns could move only by road) and protection. Designed in spring 1942 and produced from February 1943, the Panzerhaubitze Wespe ('armoured howitzer wasp') was a 105mm leichte Feldhaubitze 18 mounted on the PzKpfw II chassis. In 1943, 518 of them were built along with some 100 examples of the Panzerhaubitze Hummel ('armoured bumble bee'), a 150mm schwere Feldhaubitze 18 mounted on a PzKpfw IV chassis, which were produced up to May 1943. Both saw their first use at the Battle of Kursk.

Infantry weapons were also improved during these years. After the poor performance in 1941 of the Mauser Gewehr 41 semi-automatic rifle, from August 1942 the successful Gewehr 41 semi-automatic produced by Walther entered mass production with 6,778 examples produced during the year and an impressive 91,597 examples produced in 1943. Also in 1942 a new machine gun entered mass production, the renowned MG 42 (17,915 produced in 1942, 116,725 in 1943) that could fire up to 1,200 rounds per minute compared with the 900 rounds fired by the older MG 34. This improvement in infantry firearms was not matched by an improvement in

Schützen await the order to move forwards while a 50mm PAK 38 fires against an enemy target. Capable of penetrating 60mm-thick, 30-degree sloping armour at a range of 500m, the PAK 38 had a very high rate of fire (14 rounds per minute) and a very low silhouette, making it a very effective weapon – though not enough to deal with the Soviet T-34 and the KV tanks.

An early production Marder II, armed with a captured Soviet 76.2mm gun on a PzKpfw II mount. Production began in April 1942, and by June 1943 some 200 examples had rolled off the lines. This self-propelled anti-tank gun was a stopgap solution aimed at levelling the playing field between German and Soviet armour. With its high silhouette and thin armour, it was mainly used as a defensive weapon.

anti-tank weapons. In 1941 it was clear that the old anti-tank rifles were no longer of any use against Soviet armour, and production of the Panzerbüchse 39 ceased in 1941 with the last 29,587 examples. At 229kg, the new carriage-mounted schwere Panzerbüchse 41, though effective, was a heavy and impractical weapon, and it never entered mass production. Only 94 examples were produced from August 1940 followed by a further 349 in 1941, 1,030 in 1942 and 1,324 in 1943 when production was halted. The only practical solution found to enable infantrymen to take on Soviet tanks was the development of a magnetic hollow-charge hand grenade, the Hoftholladung 3 HL, which weighed 3kg and could penetrate as much as 140mm of armour; 8,500 were produced in 1942, followed by another 358,400 in 1943. Other improvements were seen in motor transport due to the production of the Raupenschlepper Ost ('tracked prime mover east'), developed after the captured Soviet tracked prime mover Stalinez 65; 1,454 examples were produced in 1942 with a further 14,012 in 1943, belatedly providing the German Army with a perfectly suitable vehicle capable of moving and towing on all roads and in any conditions. The fact that Panzer Divisions were not given top priority in its allocation is just another indication of how things had changed since the blitzkrieg years.

Panzergrenadiers reach the railway leading to central Stalingrad, thus breaking through the city's western defence line. The mixed use of the SdKfz 251 (designed to carry 12 men) and the SdKfz 250 (carrying six) became common in the Schützen/Panzergrenadier Kompanie following the 1 November 1941 reorganization.

Command, control, communications and intelligence

Auftragstaktik: the German mission command system at work

One explanation of how the Panzer Divisions could, and most often did, overcome their enemies despite the unfavourable odds against them lies in their unique command system. This was actually common to the entire German Army but was better implemented in the divisions' fast and mobile units. The Auftragstaktik (literally, 'mission tactic' – though it was not a tactic at all), was a command system based on the devolution of command in the field from senior commanders to their subordinates, at every level. In practice, a unit commander would not be told how to achieve his task, but rather just what his task was; it was then up to him to find the most suitable way to deal with the conditions encountered on the battlefield. Thus the Panzer Divisions were able to move quickly towards their assigned objectives, and were capable of reacting promptly to any unexpected developments on the battlefield. Auftragstaktik lay at the heart of the German concepts of manoeuvre and flexibility; even though some kind of basic plan was always laid down on maps, this could be easily and quickly changed to meet any unavoidable problems on the battlefield.

The actual implementation plan in a 'real' Panzer Division moving toward its assigned target was, of course, much more complicated than this may suggest. The first step lay at the corps/division command level. Once the corps/division commander had selected the march routes and the assigned targets for each of the divisions under his control, the Panzer Division's command staff (Stab) would work out the detail and select the march routes and the targets for each designated combat element. Basic guidelines were given by the Divisionskommandeur (divisional commander) and subsequently worked out by the operations officer, the Ia. March routes were selected and a Marschgruppe (march group) was assigned to each one, taking into account the information on enemy dispositions that the divisional intelligence officer, the Ic, had been able to provide (not an easy task when the divisions were on the move). The march group, which would eventually become the Kampfgruppe, or combat group, was made up of a specific unit selected for a given route and

Two armoured cars abandoned during the Soviet counter-offensive of winter 1941/42: to the left, an eight-wheeled SdKfz 232 schwere Panzerspähwagen Funk (heavy radio armoured car), and to the right, a leichte SdKfz 222 four-wheeled Panzerspähwagen. The lack of armoured cars, both light and heavy, in the Panzer Divisions was mitigated only by the use of the SdKfz 250 light half-track.

target. In 1940 these groups were formed by the main elements of the division, which were the Panzer Brigade (the spearhead units) and the Schützen Brigade (the main support unit), supported by the Panzerjäger and the Pionier battalions. However, experience gained in the 1940 campaign in the West showed that such a breakdown was no longer the best solution.

In 1941 the various units of a Panzer Division were broken down and arranged to form composite march and combat groups, which did not require support from other elements, eventually enabling them to move and fight in a faster way than before. Thus, for example, the former spearhead (the Panzer Brigade) was now replaced by a composite Kampfgruppe made up of the Panzer Regiment (either two or three Abteilungen), the half-track-mounted Schützen units (companies or a battalion, if available), one or more artillery battalions plus companies detached from the Panzerjäger and the Panzer Pionier battalions. Therefore, the Kampfgruppe would not need to call for artillery support or for the intervention of the Schützen, the Panzerjäger and the Pionier units even in worst-case scenarios. Movement was essential when forming these Kampfgruppen, which explains why in general only those Schützen units mounted on the Schützenpanzerwagen were considered suitable for accompanying the Panzers, whose movement they actually matched (the same applied to the Panzer Pionier units, especially to the third armoured company of the battalion). One or more support groups, intended either to advance in support of the spearhead or to follow it up, could be formed by the Schützen Brigade and the Panzer Aufklärungs Abteilung; the latter, generally speaking, used to reconnoitre the Panzer Divisions' axis of advance.

Each Kampfgruppe was put under command of either a brigade or a regimental commander, who would be given the assigned march route and the target by the divisional Stab. This was most commonly a place, a town or a river crossing that was intended to be seized before undertaking the following step in the divisional advance. In turn, the Kampfgruppe commander would issue his own specific orders to the commanders of the units he had at that moment under his command (regardless of whether they had been temporarily attached). This too was done following the Auftragstaktik system. Every commander was to concern himself only with his own given route and target; others would take care of any problem or issue that might arise elsewhere.

In combat, commanders at every level were required to react promptly and to issue orders very quickly, verbally if possible. The Germans rule was that it was always better to issue an incomplete order quickly than to issue a complete and detailed order that took a long time. At the Kampfgruppe level, the

A mixed Kampfgruppe of Panzer Regiment 6 and Schützen Regiment 3, both of 3. Panzer Division, spearheads the advance of Guderian's Panzergruppe 2 on its way to Roslavl, July 1941. The command pennant sported by the Kfz 15 command car on the left denotes it belonging to a Schützen Regiment Stab,. In this case it is being supported by a leichte Panzerzug with an SdKfz 223 radio armoured car detached from Nachrichten Abteilung 39.

commander was required to evaluate the situation quickly; then he would give his orders to the subordinate units, again following the Auftragstaktik system. Battalion or company commanders would be told what they were required to do: either to advance in a determined direction to meet the enemy or to take a position to lay down fire at him. He would be allowed a free hand in how to perform his tasks. Thus, for example, a Panzer Regiment commander in charge of a Kampfgruppe made up of the above-mentioned units could instruct his Panzer Abteilung to advance in a given direction while the Schützen, with the support of the Panzerjäger and Pionier units, would engage the enemy under artillery support. Then, it was the task of the individual commanders to see how they could best execute their orders. A factor not to be underrated was the need to maintain links with the higher command (in this case the divisional Stab and the Divisionskommandeur) to keep them abreast of the evolving situation and what actions would be taken to accomplish any objective.

The 'lead forward' concept

German commanders were required, at almost every level, to 'lead forward', that is, to maintain contact with their subordinate units and to move together with them in order to understand the situation in the most accurate, detailed and efficient manner. This enabled them to react quickly, even when facing unexpected situations, which in the German mental framework was the rule on the battlefield. Control formed the core of the Auftragstaktik at both divisional and brigade/regimental level (to limit ourselves to this specific area). Just as the Divisionskommandeur and his Stab had to be kept continuously informed of how the situation on the battlefield was evolving, so did the Kampfgruppe commander with the units he had under command. Only in this way could he appreciate the situation and issue his own orders, either with the aim of accomplishing his part of the task or to meet any unexpected development. Communications played a major role in this field. The lowest echelon of long-range communication was the battalion's Nachrichten Zug, or communications platoon. In general, it was made up of two lorry- or half-track-mounted radio sections (Funktrupps), pack radio sections (Tornister Funktrupps – two for every company in the battalion) and a lorry- or half-track-mounted telephone section (Fernsprechtrupp), only used when the unit was not on the move (AFV-mounted units only used the Funktrupp for inward and outward communication). The

A group of officers, probably belonging to the Stab of a Panzer Abteilung, awaits the arrival of their regimental commander beside a Befehls Panzer III. After discussing the situation on the ground with these men, and making his own assessment, the commander would then issue his orders.

system worked in a very simple way; each pack radio section (carried on any available motor transport) was detached to each company with one section retained at battalion HQ, maintaining a direct link with the higher HQ – regiment, Kampfgruppe and even divisional HQ. Also, one section remained with the battalion HQ while the other one was detached to the higher HQ. Thus, communications were on a direct line between the higher HQ, the battalion HQ and its subordinate companies. When required, either because the Kampfgruppe had no Nachrichten Zug of its own or because improved communications were needed, a Nachrichten Zug could be detached from the Nachrichten Abteilung to establish a direct link (or even to increase the means of communication) with the group or subordinate HQ, if not directly to a subunit performing a specific task.

However, communication problems still arose. The available radio systems (in particular the pack radio sets) often had inadequate range, making it impossible to keep contact with the battalion HQ. To improve the actual range, the Germans used Morse code. Such messages had to be enciphered in order to prevent the enemy from understanding them, which often meant long delays until the deciphered messages could be read. To aid in this, simple codes were developed that, along with the improvements in radio apparatus (especially those carried on tanks and vehicles used by the Nachrichten Zug), eventually enabled German commanders to obtain information and to issue their

A late-production SdKfz 141 Panzer Befehlswagen III armed with a 50mm KwK L/42 and featuring Schürzen ('apron') turret armour, winter 1942/43. This model was produced from August 1942 in small numbers (only 81 examples were produced up to November 1942 with a further 104 converted between March and September 1943). It was intended to make good the lack of armament of the Panzer Befehlswagen. In converted versions of this vehicle the frame antenna on the back was replaced by a six-rod antenna.

orders very quickly. Often communications would break down in combat, especially when crossing rivers or under enemy fire. Messengers were the only alternative, despite their slowness. A first consequence of this was that forward units were often exposed to friendly fire, especially from the air. Until the Panzer Funk Kompanien were reorganized in June 1942, the Panzer Divisions could only signal to air units using flags or prearranged signs made with sheets. Later, a Flieger Verbindungs Offizier communication section was created in their fourth platoon. Secondly, a commander's capacity to evaluate the situation and subsequently to give his own orders was restricted and impeded. The 'lead forward' concept was intended to make good these shortcomings.

Speed was of the essence, and, as the Germans believed that wasting time meant losing the battle, this system eventually enabled commanders at every level to avoid sluggish, long-distance communications involving several intermediate steps before a report or an order reached its destination. It also helped close the gap between how a situation was reported and the way it could be understood when not on the spot. This was of course a double-edged sword, given the very high casualty rates suffered by German officers during the war, of almost every rank. Yet it was a system that, along with the Auftragstaktik and the skills of most of the German commanders, eventually enabled the Panzer Divisions to maintain an edge over the enemy.

Leading a Panzer Division on the battlefield

Speed, manoeuvre and flexibility were the key factors that enabled the Panzer Divisions to win their battles during the rapid advances of the early war. The implementation of these on the battlefield was made possible by the German command system, which had in Auftragstaktik and the 'lead forward' concepts two highly efficient tools. In practice, a Panzer Division on the battlefield was divided into a series of different Kampfgruppe, each one behaving independently, focusing exclusively on its own task and ignoring all else. Every Kampfgruppe commander was to take care of his own assigned route and target, determining how best to attain it and, by keeping in close contact with his subordinate units, how to deal with any unexpected situations. Unless directly threatened, he was not to concern himself with his flanks and rear and, above all, he was not to concern himself with what other Kampfgruppen were doing. This was a task reserved for the Divisionskommandeur.

Supported by his Stab, the Divisionskommandeur was the only one intended to have a complete picture of the situation on the entire divisiononal front. He could give direct orders to the Kampfgruppe commanders to help them deal

Command and control in action

PHASE 1:
Divisional commander arranges the Marschgruppe (March Groups) and issues orders to their commanders. Each group is formed around a regimental HQ and is made up of a mixture of main combat elements plus artillery and support elements. Group A, under command of the Panzer Regiment HQ, represents the armoured (main) attack group and will advance along the main route, while Group B will secure the divisional northern shoulder. Group C has orders to reconnoitre the divisional southern shoulder and to link up with neighbouring units, also serving as a reserve group.

PHASE 2:
Contact with the enemy; Group B attacks and seizes enemy-held positions while Group A meets stronger enemy forces. The two Panzer Abteilung succeed in getting through, but the infantry gets stuck.

PHASE 3:
Commander of Group A decides to move on and orders the Panzer Regiment to continue its advance, leaving infantry to mop up the area; he informs the divisional commander. Since no more enemy activity is seen in the area of Group B, its commander sends the Kradschützen Bataillon to probe forward. Meanwhile, the Aufklärungs Abteilung continues its march.

PHASE 4:
Using the situation reports coming from the group commanders and after talking with the commander of Group A, the divisional commander assesses the situation and issues his orders; the Panzer Regiment must continue its advance, now supported by one infantry battalion detached from Group B. Also, he approves orders issued by Group B commander, leaving the Kradschützen Bataillon to probe forward while the infantry battalion continues to secure the area. Since the Aufklärungs Abteilung has established contact with friendly forces, the infantry battalion from Group C is sent to help the infantry of Group A in the mopping up of the area. Their advance will be resumed as soon as possible.

Auftragstaktik in action

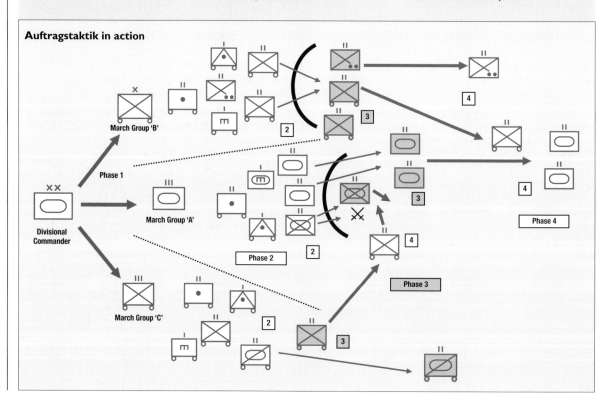

80

with the situation they were actually facing on the basis of his knowledge of the bigger picture. Yet in a general way the Divisionskommandeur would only intervene if a position held by his subordinate units was endangered or if a situation could be exploited by switching units from other Kampfgruppen, which could not be attaine by moving an entire Kampfgruppe from elsewhere. Speed, manoeuvrability and flexibility would be assured with the higher commanders dealing with the overall conditions on the battlefield. The system worked practically at every level, from the battalion upwards, yet it was at the divisional level that control required the greatest care and attention, since any failure at this level could affect the division as a whole.

In 1942 the Stab of a Panzer Division was neither large nor cumbersome. In total it was only 61 strong, including 17 officers, 11 officials (Beamten), 17 non-commissioned officers and 16 other ranks. The actual command echelon, directly entrusted with the task of leading the division on the battlefield, was even smaller and included, other than the Divisionskommandeur and his orderly, only three officers, two NCOs and one other ranks in the operations department (Ia) and four officers, one NCO and three other ranks in the intelligence department (Ic). They would form the advanced command detachment, Führungs Staffel, which had the task of leading forward the combat elements of the Panzer Division while the logistics detachment (Quartiermeister) followed up with the divisional rear and supply units. Most interestingly, the Führungs Staffel was a small unit that borrowed communications vehicles, either half-tracks or armoured cars, from the Panzer Nachrichten Zug and possibly some AFVs used for self-defence from other units such as the Panzer Aufklärungs Abteilung (only in North Africa was the Führungs Staffel organized as a full combat unit). In 1941, 13. Panzer Division's Führungs Staffel included two small cars, four command cars and one truck, carrying nine officers, eight NCOs and a dozen other ranks.

These small command detachments moved closely, following up the spearheading march and battle groups, establishing a command post in a suitable position and maintaining contact with the single commanders and the divisional rear and supply units. When needed, the commander himself would lead forward, joining the groups, talking to their commanders and assessing the situation at first hand, putting him in position to make the right decision at the right moment. Seeing their commanders on the battlefield in the heat of battle also served as a boost to the morale of the soldiers, especially when facing overwhelming odds. Yet the command system soon turned into a critical issue for the Panzer Divisions. Heavily relying on skilled and capable unit commanders at almost every level, not to mention the skilled and well-trained men supporting them (in the field of communications, as one example alone), the Panzer Divisions would feel the shortages of such men following the heavy losses suffered in the winters of 1941/42 and 1942/43, a situation further aggravated by the rapid growth in the number of the Panzer Divisions. As the war went on, it became more difficult to keep up with the standards of the blitzkrieg years, and the Panzer Divisions' command system would eventually turn towards the direct control of subordinate units by higher commanders.

Unit status

A headquarters unit of 7. Panzer Division, with an SdKfz 260/261 kleine Panzerfunkwagen (small radio car) detached from Nachrichten Abteilung 83, moves through a Soviet village. The original caption indicates this is a major road, showing how difficult conditions could be in the wet.

Motor vehicles belonging to the second leichte Panzer Kompanie of an unknown Panzer Abteilung move at full speed on a Soviet road, passing two destroyed KV I tanks during Operation *Barbarossa*. The presence of Soviet heavy tanks, such as the KVs and the T-34, caught the German Army by surprise.

The reorganization of the Panzer Divisions that began in summer 1940 lasted all through the following autumn and winter, and was only completed just before the beginning of *Barbarossa*. In August 1940 only two of the four divisions planned were actually created, 11. Panzer Division (formed 1 August 1940 with elements of 4 and 231. Infanterie Division, with Panzer Regiment 15 from 5. Panzer Division from September) and 14. Panzer Division (formed 15 August but renamed as such on 12 December, with Panzer Regiment 36 from 4. Panzer Division from November). Four other divisions were formed in October: 12. Panzer Division on the 5th, from 2. Infanterie Division (mot); 13. Panzer Division on the 11th, from 13. Infanterie Division (mot) plus Panzer Regiment 4 from 2. Panzer Division; 20. Panzer Division on the 20th, from elements of 19. Infanterie Division; and 18. Panzer Division on the 26th, from elements of 4 and 14. Infanterie Divisions. The last group came on 1 November 1940 with 15. Panzer Division (from 33. Infanterie Division, eventually sent to North Africa), 16. Panzer Division (from 16. Infanterie Division and elements of 6. Panzer Division plus Panzer Regiment 2 of 1. Panzer Division), 17. Panzer Division (from 27. Infanterie Division) and 19. Panzer Division (formed from 19. Infanterie Division). Most of the old Panzer Divisions also underwent major reorganization; 1. Panzer Division, which gave its Panzer Regiment 2 to 16. Panzer Division in October 1940, in November formed Schützen Regiment 113 which, like SR 1, had one SPW-mounted battalion. 2. Panzer Division followed a similar path; in October it gave its Panzer Regiment 4 to 13. Panzer Division and added Schützen Regiment 304; 3. Panzer Division underwent major changes, having formed Schützen Regiment 394 in November 1940, and in January 1941 gave its Panzer Regiment 5, Panzer Aufklärungs Abteilung 5, Panzerjäger Abteilung 39 and I./Artillerie Regiment 75 to the newly forming 5. leichte Division (eventually to become on 1 August 1941 21. Panzer Division in North Africa). As a replacement the division received in February–March I. Abteilung of Panzer Regiment 28 (formerly with 18. Panzer Division, equipped with Tauch-Panzer, the 'swimming' PzKpfw III; it became III./Panzer Regiment 6), the II./Artillerie Regiment 49, Panzer Aufklärungs Abteilung 1 and Panzerjäger Abteilung 543. On 1 March 18. Panzer Division's Panzer Regiment 28 was disbanded and replaced by Panzer Regiment 18, whose third Abteilung came from III./PzRgt 28.

4. Panzer Division, which gave its Panzer Regiment 36 to 14. Panzer Division in November 1940, formed Kradschützen Bataillon 34 and the Schützen Regiment 33 in January 1941, as well as bringing each Abteilung of its Panzer Regiment 35 up to four companies and adding a third Abteilung to its Artillerie Regiment 103 and an SIG Kompanie to both its Schützen Regiments. 5. Panzer Division gave its Panzer Regiment 15 to 11. Panzer Division and, in August 1940, formed Kradschützen Bataillon 55, while 6. Panzer Division

formed its Schützen Regiment 114. 7. Panzer Division added a third Abteilung to its Artillerie Regiment 78 in January 1941, while its Panzer Abteilung 66 was officially renamed III./Panzer Regiment 25. Likewise, Panzer Abteilung 67 of 8. Panzer Division became III./Panzer Regiment 10 in January 1941, while a new Schützen Regiment 28 was also formed and a third Abteilung was added to Artillerie Regiment 80. In the same month 10. Panzer Division gave its Panzer Regiment 8 to 15. Panzer Division, formed Kradschützen Bataillon 10 and added a third Abteilung to Artillerie Regiment 90. There was no major change for 9. Panzer Division.

Most of the divisions completed their reorganization in early 1941, with both 18 and 20. Panzer doing so by May. By then, the reorganized Panzerwaffe was already back at war. In April 1941 six Panzer Divisions took part in the invasion of Yugoslavia and Greece, four (8, 9, 11 and 14) of which were soon redeployed for *Barbarossa,* while two others (2 and 5) were sent back to Germany and held in reserve. 12. Panzer Division was held in reserve for the Balkans but took no part in that campaign, while in May 5. Panzer Division was intended to be sent to North Africa. In June 1941 there were 17 Panzer Divisions deployed for *Barbarossa,* divided between four newly formed Panzergruppen, the equivalent of an armoured army: Panzergruppe 1 (Generaloberst Ewald von Kleist) in the Heeres Gruppe Süd area had three motorized army corps with a total of five Panzer Divisions (9, Generalleutnant Alfred von Hubicki; 11, Generalmajor Ludwig Crüwell until August, then Generalmajor Hans-Karl von Esebeck until October and Generalmajor Walter Scheller after that; 13, Generalmajor Walter Düvert until December then Generalmajor Traugott Herr; 14, Generalmajor Friedrich Kühn; and 16, Generalmajor Hans Valentin Hube), while Panzergruppe 4 (Generaloberst Erich Hoepner) in the Heeres Gruppe Nord area had only two corps with three Panzer Divisions (1, Generalmajor Friedrich Kirchner until 16 July then Generalmajor Walter Krüger; 6, Generalmajor Franz Landgraf until November then Generalmajor Erhard Raus; 8, Generalmajor Erich Brandenberger until December, then back in March 1942 and temporarily replaced by Generalmajor Werner Hühner).

The stronger group was in the Heeres Gruppe Mitte area, with Panzergruppe 2 (Generaloberst Heinz Guderian) with three corps and five Panzer Divisions (3, Generalleutnant Walter Model until October then Generalmajor Hermann Breith; 4, Generalmajor Willibald von Langermann und Erlencamp until December then Generalmajor Heinrich Eberbach; 10, Generalleutnant Ferdinand Schaal until 2 August then Generalmajor Wolfgang Fischer; 17, Oberst Karl von Weber until 17 July then Generalmajor Wilhelm von Thoma, Generalleutnant Hans-Jürgen von Arnim from 15 September and Oberst Rudolf-Eduard Licht from 11 November; 18, Generalmajor Walther Nehring), while Panzergruppe 3 (General der Infanterie Hermann Hoth until 4 October, then General der Panzertruppen Georg-Hans Reinhardt) had two corps with four Panzer Divisions (7, Generalmajor Hans von Funck; 12, Generalmajor Josef Harpe; 19, Generalmajor Otto von Knobelsdorff; 20, Generalmajor Horst Stumpff until 13 October and then Generalmajor Wilhelm von Thoma). During summer 1941 there were a few minor changes to divisional organization: 17. Panzer Division's

The PzKpfw IV Ausf F was the last version to mount the 75mm KwK 37 L/24 gun, though its improved armour (up to 50mm thick) enabled it to better deal with Soviet anti-tank guns. After the last 25 examples had been upgunned in March 1942 with the 75mm KwK 40 L/43 gun, production ceased and this version was renamed the FI. In the background are two ADZG Polizei Panzerkampfwagen, 25 of which were produced in early 1942 for use by the German military police on the Eastern Front.

Schützen fire on an enemy-held position. The soldier in the foreground is armed with an MG 34 machine gun, and the troops are supported by a 20mm Flak 30 gun-armed SdKfz 10/4 self-propelled anti-aircraft half-track. The latter equipped the Fla Kompanie attached to the Panzerjäger Abteilung in 1941, and was a widely used anti-aircraft weapon. However, in 1942 the need for improved protection led to the attachment of the 88mm-armed Heeres Flak Artillerie Abteilung.

Until the appointment on 28 February 1943 of Heinz Guderian as Generalinspekteur der Panzertruppen (general inspector of armoured troops) no organic plan had existed of how the organization of the Panzer Divisions should evolve. Up to this point, it had been the responsibility of the General der Schnellen Truppen beim Oberbefehlshaber des Heeres (general of the fast troops by the C-in-C of the army); despite several key personalities holding the position, it never really functioned as a role. The first to hold this position was Wilhelm von Thoma; a Panzer Division field commander, he delegated most of the job to his successor Oberst (from 1 August Generalmajor) Hermann Breith, who took over on 1 July 1941. Oberst Hermann Balck (promoted to Generalmajor on 1 August 1942), in charge between November 1941 and May 1942 (with von Thoma back in command until August), was an excellent commander but could do little or nothing to change the status quo. The same applied to the last man to hold the position, Oberst (Generalmajor from 1 November 1942) Hans Cramer. Guderian was the first to obtain full powers and direct subordination to Hitler, enabling him to influence the organization of the divisions.

III./Panzer Regiment 39 (Tauch-Panzer, attached on 1 June) was detached on 16 August thus leaving the division with only two Panzer Abteilungen, like 19. Panzer Division's Panzer Regiment 27 whose III Abteilung was disbanded on 10 August. Also in August, 12. Panzer Division's Panzer Aufklärungs Abteilung 2 and Kradschützen Bataillon 22 were merged together to form the Voraus Abteilung 2 (advanced detachment); PzAufklAbt 2 was eventually disbanded on 27 November, its remnants absorbed by the Kradschützen Bataillon 22. 16. Panzer Division's PzAufklAbt 16 was also disbanded in September and its remnants were absorbed by Kradschützen Bataillon 16. This would herald the reorganization of the reconnaissance elements: both 2 and 5. Panzer Divisions lost their Panzer Aufklärungs Abteilung (PzAufklAbt 5 disbanded on 11 August, PzAufklAbt 8 detached from 5 to 23. Panzer Division as Kradschützen Bataillon 23 on 13 September), while their Kradschützen Bataillone were reorganized, adding a Panzer Späh Kompanie. Other divisions followed before the end of the year: 11. Panzer Division's PzAufklAbt 231 was disbanded and absorbed by Kradschützen Bataillon 61 on 1 December, and on 21 December 18. Panzer Division's PzAufklAbt 88 suffered the same fate after it had already been merged with Kradschützen Bataillon 18 in November. Between September and October a major reshuffle also took place at the front with Panzergruppe 4 transferred to the Heeres Gruppe Mitte, as 9 and 11. Panzer Divisions were also transferred from Panzergruppe 1, while both 2 and 5. Panzer Divisions were sent to the Eastern Front to take part in Operation *Taifun*.

In 1941 further Panzer Divisions (beyond 21. Panzer Division) were formed: 22. Panzer Division was formed on 25 September using Panzer Regiment 204, 23. Panzer Division on 21 September with Panzer Brigade 101, and on 28 November 1941 24. Panzer Division was formed from 1. Kavallerie Division. Two more divisions would be formed in 1942 (25 in Norway on 25 February and 26 from 23. Infanterie Division on 14 September), plus 27. Panzer Division on the field. A major reorganization took place in spring 1942. All other Panzer Divisions reorganized their Panzer Aufklärungs Abteilung/Kradschützen Battailon according to the 'Panzer Division 42' organization (8. Panzer Division in January; 4 and 9 in March; 1, 3, 13, 14 and 17 in April; 19 and 20 in May; 6 and 7 in June), while the divisions in the northern and central part of the front handed over some of their Panzer Abteilungen to those in the south preparing for the new offensive. Some went to the motorized divisions: 1. Panzer Division's I./PzRgt 1 became Panzer Abteilung 16 of the 16. Infanterie Division (mot) on 26 May, 17. Panzer Division's I./PzRgt 39 became 29. Infanterie Division's Panzer Abteilung 129

Red Army soldiers surrender to a motorized artillery column, July 1941; the AFV in the background is an SdKfz 253 artillery observation vehicle. The insignia of 1. Panzer Division can just be made out.

on 19 June, 18. Panzer Division's III./PzRgt 18 became 3. Infanterie Division's Panzer Abteilung 103 on 5 April (it had already absorbed the remnants of Panzer Flamm Abteilung 100 in March) while I./PzRgt 18 became 60. Infanterie Division's Panzer Abteilung 160 on 15 June (II./PzRgt 18 was therefore renamed Panzer Abteilung 18 and the regimental Stab was disbanded). Other divisions transferred their armour to sister units: 2. Panzer Division's I./PzRgt 3 became 9. Panzer Division's III./PzRgt 33 on 10 May, 4. Panzer Division's II./PzRgt 35 became 11. Panzer Division's III./PzRgt 15 on 19 June, 8. Panzer Division's II./PzRgt 10 became 16. Panzer Division's III./PzRgt 2 on 28 May (Stab and III./PzRgt 10 were detached on 16 September leaving the division with a single Abteilung), 10. Panzer Division's I./PzRgt 7 became 14. Panzer Division's III./PzRgt 36 on 2 June, 12. Panzer Division's III./PzRgt 29 became 13. Panzer Division's III./PzRgt 4 on 15 May. Two divisions just lost part of their armour due to losses; 19. Panzer Division's I./PzRgt 27 was disbanded on 31 March and replaced by the II Abteilung which took its number, while 20. Panzer Division's I and II./PzRgt 21 were disbanded in June after they had already handed over all remaining tanks to the III./PzRgt 21 which, following the disbandment of the regimental Stab on 26 April, was renamed Panzer Abteilung 21 on 25 June.

Owing to losses, three divisions were withdrawn from the front and sent to France to rest and refit: 6. Panzer Division in April (in June its Panzer Abteilung 65 was disbanded like the PzAufklAbt 57, their remnants absorbed by Panzer Regiment 11 and Kradschützen Bataillon 6), followed in May by 7. Panzer Division (whose III./PzRgt 25 had already been disbanded on 15 March) and 10. Panzer Division, eventually sent to Tunisia the following December. Other changes included the attachment to the Panzer Divisions of a Heeres Flak Artillerie Abteilung, often as the IV./Artillerie Regiment, and the reorganization of Schützen units, renamed Panzergrenadier on 5 July and now equipped to a larger extent with SPWs. Even the newly formed divisions sent to the Eastern Front were reorganized: in April, 22. Panzer Division added a third Abteilung to its Panzer Regiment 204, which 23. Panzer Division's Panzer Regiment 201 had already done on 2 February. In June 1942, on paper the Panzerwaffe was stronger than ever with its five Panzer armies (four of which were on the Eastern Front), its 12 Panzer Korps (created by renaming the motorized corps between 24 June and 4 July; 11 were on the Eastern Front) and its 25 Panzer Divisions. Yet, only 11 of these were fully operational, two being in North Africa and the other nine in the southern part of the Eastern Front (3, Generalmajor Franz Westoven since October; 9, Oberst Johannes Basler April up to July, then Generalmajor Heinrich-Hermann von Hülsen; 11, Hermann Balck until March 1943, then Generalleutnant Dietrich von Choltitz until May and Generalmajor Johann Mickl later on; 13, Oberst Wilhelm Crisolli until May 1943, then Generalleutnant Helmuth von der Chevallerie; 14, Generalmajor Ferdinand Heim July to October, Oberst Martin Lattmann from November; 16, Generalmajor Gunther Argern from September; 22, Generalmajor Wilhelm von Apell until October, Oberst Erich Rodt from November 1942; 23, Generalmajor Hans von Boineburg-Lengsfeld until December then Oberst, later Generalmajor, Nikolaus von Vormann; 24, Generalmajor Bruno von Hauenschild, from September Generalmajor Arno von Lenski). Another ten divisions were only partly operational or just fit for defence (1, Generalmajor Walter Krüger; 2, Generalmajor Rudolf Veiel until

The Panzer Späh Kompanie of a Kradschützen Bataillon reconnoitres a town deep in the Caucasus region of the Soviet Union, summer 1942. The first and third armoured cars are SdKfz 221 leichte Panzerspähwagen while the second is an SdKfz 223 light radio armoured car. Both were widely used until late in the war.

27. Panzer Division

The creation of 27. Panzer Division was an experiment aimed at evaluating how a field unit could perform after it had been formed without any prior training. The unit was created on 1 September 1942 using elements from 22. Panzer Division's 'Gruppe Michalik' made of Panzergrenadier Regiment 140 and III./PzRgt 204 (renamed Panzer Abteilung 127), plus the I./Artillerie Regiment 140 (renamed I./Artillerie Regiment 127), elements from the Kradschützen Bataillon 24 and army units (Panzerjäger Abteilung 560 then 127, Pionier Bataillon 260 then 127, II./Artillerie Regiment 51 then 127 and the new Panzer Aufklärungs Abteilung 127). The division was about only 3,000 strong, but it was split into more Kampfgruppen and used against Soviet spearheads in the lower Don area at Voronesh and Voroshilovgrad. By early February its strength had dropped to about 1,600 and, on 15 February, the division was disbanded and its remnants were absorbed by 7. Panzer Division (remnants of Panzergrenadier Regiment 140 went to the II./PzGrenRgt 7). Oberst Helmuth Michalik was the commander until 29 November 1942, before being replaced by Oberst Hans Tröger. Many thought the units that made up the division would have been better employed with their parent divisions, and the experiment was widely seen as a failure.

In this series of photographs, an SdKfz 231 eight-wheeled heavy armoured car fires its 20mm KwK 30 against a Soviet BA-32 heavy armoured car armed with a 45mm gun. The fact that the German armoured car has the turret turned away suggests the scene was probably posed.

February 1942, then Generalmajor Hans-Karl von Esebeck; 4, Oberst Erich Schneider from November; 5, Generalmajor Gustav Fehn until September 1942, then Generalmajor Eduard Metz; 8, Generalmajor Erich Brandenberger until January 1943, then Generalmajor Sebastian Fichtner; 12, Oberst Walter Wessel January 1942 through February 1943, then Oberst, later Generalmajor, Erpo von Bodenhausen; 17, Oberst Rudolf-Eduard Licht until October 1942, then Generalmajor Frido von Senger und Etterlin; 18, Generalmajor Karl von Thüngen from January 1942, replaced by Generalmajor Erwin Menny between September and December; 19, Oberst, later Generalmajor Gustav Schmidt from January 1942; 20, Generalmajor Walter Duvert July to October 1942, then Oberst Heinrich von Lüttwitz).

The closing months of 1942 marked the high point of the Panzerwaffe; the total number of Panzer Divisions reached 27, 22 of which were on the Eastern Front. Then a decline began. In the first months of 1943 the extent of the defeat suffered at Stalingrad was clear; while in January the badly mauled 1. Panzer Division had been withdrawn from the Eastern Front and sent to France to rest and refit, three divisions were lost at Stalingrad in early February (14, 16 and 24, to be reformed in Germany) and two other divisions were disbanded during the year (27 on 15 February and 22 on 4 March, eventually followed by 18. Panzer Division on 29 September), leaving thus only 16 partly operational divisions on the Eastern Front. A further reorganization began in spring 1943; Kradschützen Bataillone were reorganized as the new Panzer Aufklärungs Abteilung, new Heeres Flak Artillerie Abteilungen were attached, other Panzergrenadier Bataillone were equipped with the SPW and the first self-propelled artillery began

Italian Bersaglieri (light infantry, left) examine a PzKpfw III Ausf H of 16. Panzer Division, part of von Kleist's Panzergruppe 1, advancing in the southern part of the Eastern Front. The Ausf H was the first version of the PzKpfw III to have the new 50mm L/42 gun as its standard main armament, though the earlier Ausf G (mounting the 37mm L/46 gun) had been retrofitted with the same gun.

to equip the Artillerie Regiment. The biggest reorganization affected the Panzer Regiments, which had their missing Abteilungen partly rebuilt and sent to Germany to be equipped with the Panther tank; 1. Panzer Division's II./PzRgt 1 became I Abteilung on 27 January and started to re-equip, while a new II./PzRgt 1 was raised from the I./PzRgt 203. 2. Panzer Division's I./PzRgt 3 was rebuilt on 25 March and started to re-equip in June, while 3. Panzer Division's III./PzRgt 6 was disbanded on 15 March and its I./PzRgt 6 started to re-equip in June as well. 5. Panzer Division's I./PzRgt 31 started to re-equip in May 1943, like 6. Panzer Division's I./PzRgt 11. 9. Panzer Division's II./PzRgt 33 was detached in January and re-equipped with the Panther to become Panzer Abteilung 51, like 11. Panzer Division's I./PzRgt 15, which was detached in February and on 15 March became Panzer Abteilung 52. It would be returned to the division on 1 September 1943, the first Panther Abteilung to join a Panzer Division (III./PzRgt 15 was disbanded then). 12. Panzer Division's I./PzRgt 29 was rebuilt on 11 May 1943; first intended to become a Tiger unit, it would begin to be re-equipped with Panthers only in July. 13. Panzer Division's III./PzRgt 4 started to re-equip in May, while both I and II Abteilung had only four Panzer Kompanien remaining. 19. Panzer Division's Panzer Regiment 27 was in better shape with its II Abteilung rebuilt on 1 April 1943, while 23. Panzer Division's III./PzRgt 201 was disbanded on 5 March, and its II Abteilung began to re-equip in April.

German Panzermänner (tankers) enjoy a song while sitting atop a PzKpfw IV Ausf G during the transfer to the Eastern Front before the Battle of Kursk, spring 1943. Following the heavy losses suffered during the first Soviet counter-offensive in winter 1941/42, numerous Panzer Divisions had to be withdrawn from the front to rest and refit in France.

A column of SdKfz 10 prime movers hauls ammunition trailers belonging to the third company of an unknown Panzerjäger Abteilung in early 1943. The use of foliage for camouflage and the MG 34s on anti-aircraft mountings were a consequence of the growing threat from Soviet air forces at this stage of the campaign.

A divisional tank park somewhere on the Eastern Front, summer 1942. On the left is a Panzer Befehlswagen III Ausf H (SdKfz 266–268) with a dummy gun and additional armour plate; in the background are two PzKpfw IV Ausf F2 armed with the long-barrelled 75mm KwK 40 L/43 gun. The turret number on the rear right (I L 7) probably denotes the seventh tank of the leichte Panzer Zug of a first Panzer Abteilung.

Lessons learned

The first stages of Operation *Barbarossa* proceeded according to plan. By July 1941 the Panzer spearheads had penetrated up to 300km into Soviet territory, inflicting some 747,870 casualties and destroying 10,180 tanks and 3,995 aircraft. By 14 October total Soviet losses amounted to some three million men, 14,196 tanks and 25,169 guns. Any other country would have collapsed, but the Soviet Union did not. However, having underestimated Soviet capabilities and given the sheer expanse of the territory, in addition to the attrition suffered by their own forces, the Germans simply failed to meet the requirements needed for their second blitzkrieg-style campaign, the one to be unleashed against Moscow. Had the Panzer Divisions replenished their losses and increased their number by more than just two new, fresh divisions, Hitler's Germany might have defeated the Soviet Union – or at least avoided the shattering defeat of winter 1941/42.

The Soviet counter-offensive of winter 1941/42 delivered a fatal blow to the German Army as a whole and to the Panzer Divisions in particular. Yet the Germans were still able to react, and by the following summer they had launched a new blitzkrieg-style campaign. The Panzer Divisions were now a blunt tool, though; their partial recovery led to their dispersion rather than to a concentration of forces which, along with the decision to have them fight alongside the infantry divisions, eventually sanctioned the end of blitzkrieg warfare.

Facing the new Soviet winter offensive of 1942–43, the Panzer Divisions proved to be no longer capable of achieving operational success on the field through offensive manoeuvres, although they achieved decisive success on the field through elastic, flexible defence. Given the improved Soviet defence capabilities and the unfavourable odds they were facing, in 1942 the

A column of PzKpfw IV Ausf G tanks on the move in the southern part of the Eastern Front, July 1943. All are equipped with hull and turret Schürzen (armour skirts) for increased protection. The leading one also has a 30mm armour plate bolted to its front hull.

Germans no longer possessed superiority in the attack and were only able to regain it in the defence. The race for better and improved weapons had started, and the Germans were lagging behind their enemies. Had the Panther tank been available in adequate numbers as early as 1942, the Panzer Divisions would probably have been able to recover some degree of offensive capability. But the fatal combination of the switch from manoeuvre to firepower, which turned the balance in favour of the latter, and of the inadequacy of available weapons eventually shattered any possible attempt.

The belated appointment of Heinz Guderian as Inspector General of the Panzertruppen (the ultimate attempt to make good the uncoordinated development of the Panzerwaffe in recent years) led to a more comprehensive and better-coordinated attempt to rebuild the divisions. Yet this attempt was not able to prevent a further dispersal of resources, the consequence of the development of Waffen-SS units and of the other independent armoured units such as those of the Tiger and Sturmgeschütze (assault guns), both defensive weapons.

In contrast to previous practice on the Eastern Front, the battle of Kursk was fought on the principle of attacking the enemy where he was strongest. Firepower had now become the decisive factor in any attack, the only one capable of achieving success on the battlefield. However,, it was the lack of adequate firepower in the Panzer Divisions that meant they could no longer achieve decisive victory.

Abbreviations and glossary

In German, a number (either Arabic or Roman) followed by a full stop denotes an ordinal number. Thus, for example, *1. Panzer Division* should read first (or *erste*) Panzer Division. Note that in German practice companies, regiments and divisions used Arabic numbers, while battalions, brigades and corps used Roman ones.

Abt	*Abteilung* (detachment, battalion)	**Ersatzteil**	spare part	**HGr, Heeresgruppe**	Army Group
AC	armoured car	**Feld**	field	**Hiwi**	*Hilfswillige* (auxiliary volunteers)
Amt	office	**Feldhaubitze**	field howitzer		
AR	*Artillerie Regiment* (artillery regiment)	**Feldersatz**	field replacement	**ID**	*Infanterie Division*
		Feldgendarmerie	military police	**IG**	*Infanterie Geschütz* (infantry gun)
Armee, AOK	Army	**Feldlazarett**	field hospital		
Art	*Artillerie* (Artillery)	**Feldpost**	field post	**Inst**	*Instandsetzung* (maintenance)
Armeekorps	Army Corps	**FH**	*Feldhaubitze* (field howitzer)		
Aufkl, Aufklärungs	reconnaissance			**IR**	*Infanterie Regiment* (infantry regiment)
		Fsp,	*Fernsprech* (telephone)		
Ausbildung	training			**K**	*kurz* (short, refers to tank guns)
Ausf	*Ausführung* (variant)	**Fl, Flamm, Flammenwerfer**	flame-thrower		
Barbarossa	German attack plan against the Soviet Union, 1941	**Fla**	*Flieger Abwehr* (anti-aircraft, used for Army AA units)	**K, Krdschtz**	*Kradschützen* (motorcycle infantry)
				Kanone	gun
Beamte	civilian official serving in military units	**Flak**	*Flieger Abwehr Kanone* (anti-aircraft artillery)	**Kartenstelle**	mapping detachment
				Kdr, Kdt	*Kommandeur/ Kommandant* (commander)
Beobachtung	observation	**Flakartillerie**	AA artillery		
Betriebsstoff	fuel (petrol)	**Funk**	radio	**Kfz**	*Kraftfahrzeug* (vehicle)
Brig	brigade	**Funktrupp**	radio section		
Brüko	*Brücken Kolonne* (bridging column)	**GD**	*Grossdeutschland* ('greater Germany', the name of an elite infantry regiment)	**KG, KGr**	*Kampfgruppe* (battle group)
Bt, Bttr	*Batterie* (battery)			**KoDiNa**	*Kommandeur Divisions Nachschubtruppen* (commander of divisional supply troops)
Btl, Batl	*Bataillon* (battalion)				
Dienst	service	**Gds**	guards		
DiNaFü	*Divisions Nachschub Führer* (divisional commander of supply units)	**Gep, gepanzert**	armoured		
		Geschütz	gun		
		Geschützstaffel	gun section (artillery)	**Kol, Kolonne**	column
		Gewehr	rifle	**Kommando**	divisional headquarters
Div	*Division, Divisions* (division, divisional)	**Gruppe**	group (used for Panzer commands at corps level, such as 'Gruppe Guderian')		
				Kp, Komp, Kompanie	company
Druckerei	printing				
DVA	*Divisions Verpflegungsamt* (divisional food supply office)	**GrW, Granatenwerfer**	mortar	**Kradm, Kradmelder**	messenger
				Kradschützen	motorcycle infantry
		H	*Heer* (army)	**Kraftfahr/ Kraftfahrzeug**	vehicle
Ergz, Ergänzung	support	**H-Flak Abt**	*Heeres Flak Abteilung* (army AA unit)		
Ersatz	replacement			**Kraftfahrpark**	vehicle park
Ersatzheer	replacement army	**Haubitze**	howitzer		

Krankenkraftwagen	ambulance	**Panzerhaubitze**	armoured howitzer
KStN	*Kriegsstärke Nachweisung* (war establishment chart)	**Panzer Korps, Panzerkorp**	armoured corps
Kw, Kraftwagen	motor vehicle	**Panzerwaffe**	German armoured arm
KwK	*Kampfwagen Kanone* (tank gun)	**Pi, Pion**	*Pionier* (engineer, sapper)
L	*lang* (long, referred to tank guns)	**Pz**	*Panzer* (tank, armour)
L, Le, Leicht	light	**PzAufklAbt**	*Panzer Aufklärungs Abteilung* (armoured reconnaissance unit)
Landungsboot	assault boat		
Lehr	demonstration		
MG	*Maschinengewehr* (machine gun)	**PzB**	*Panzerbüchse* (anti-tank rifle)
mittler	medium	**PzBefh**	*Panzerbefehlswagen* (command tank)
mot	*motorisiert* (motorized)	**PzDiv**	*Panzer Division* (armoured division)
mot S	*motorisierte Selbstfahrlafette* (self-propelled)	**PzG, PzGren**	*Panzergrenadier* (armoured infantry, name applied to all Schützen units from 5 July 1942)
mot Z	*motorisierter Zugkraftwagen* (motorized, towed by a vehicle)		
MTW	*(gepanzerter) Mannschafts Transport Wagen* (armoured personnel carrier vehicles)	**PzJäg**	*Panzerjäger* (anti-tank)
		PzKpfw	*Panzerkampfwagen* (tank, AFV)
		PzRgt	*Panzer Regiment* (tank regiment)
Nachr, Nachrichten	communication	**PzSpäh, Panzer Späh, Panzerspäh**	armoured car
Nachschub	supply	**R**	rifle
Nb	*Nebelwerfer* (rocket launcher)	**Rgt**	*Regiment* (regiment)
		Rückwartige Dienst	rear area units
OKH	*Oberkommando des Heeres* (Army High Command)	**S, schw, Schwer**	heavy
		Sanitäts	medical
		Schlachterei	butcher
PAK	*Panzer Abwehr Kanone* (anti-tank gun)	**Schtz, Schützen**	light infantry, motorized
Panzergruppe	Panzer group, equivalent to an army	**SdKfz**	*Sondern Kraftfahrzeug* (special vehicle)

sfl	*Selbstfahrlafette* (self-propelled mount)		
SIG	*Schwere Infanterie Geschütz* (heavy infantry gun)		
SR	*Schützen Regiment* (motorized infantry regiment)		
St	*Sturm* (assault)		
St, Stab	HQ, staff		
Staffel	squadron		
(t)	*tschechisch* (Czech)		
Tauch Panzer	submersible PzKpfw III variant		
Tornister	pack		
Tross	train		
Tr, Trupp	section		
Verm	*Vermessung* (survey)		
Verpfl	*Verplegung* (administrative)		
Versorgungsdienst	supply service		
Versorgungtruppe	supply units		
Verw	*Verwaltung* (administration)		
Vorausabteilung	advanced detachment		
Wehrkreis	military district		
Werkst, Werkstatt	workshop		
Wurfrahmen	rocket launcher frame		
zbV	*zur besonderen Verwendung* (for special purposes)		
Zitadelle	attack plan against Kursk, 1943		
Zug	platoon		

Officers' ranks equivalents

Leutnant	Lieutenant	**Generalleutnant**	(Brigadier)/one-star General
Oberleutnant	First Lieutenant	**Generalmajor**	Lieutenant General/two-star
Hauptmann	Captain	**General, General der...**	Major General/three-star General
Major	Major	**Generaloberst**	General/four-star General
Oberstleutnant	Lieutenant Colonel	**Generalfeldmarschall**	Field Marshal
Oberst	Colonel		

Bibliography

Bonn, Keith (editor) *Slaughterhouse. The Handbook of the Eastern Front* (Bedford, PA: Aberjona, 2005)

Chamberlain, Peter and Hilary L. Doyle *Encyclopedia of German Tanks of World War Two* (London: Arms and Armour, 1978)

Citino, Robert M. *Death of the Wehrmacht. The German Campaigns of 1942* (Lawrence, KS: University Press of Kansas, 2007)

Dunnigan, James F. (editor) *The Russian Front. Germany's War in the East, 1941-45* (London: Arms & Armour Press, 1978)

Fugate, Bryan *Operation Barbarossa. Strategy and Tactics on the Eastern Front, 1941* (Novato, CA: Presidio Press, 1984)

Glantz, David M. (editor) *The Initial Period of War on the Eastern Front, 22 June–August 1941* (London – Portland, OR: Frank Cass, 1993)

—— *When Titans Clashed: How the Red Army Stopped Hitler* (Lawrence, KS: University Press of Kansas, 1995)

—— *Kharkov 1942. Anatomy of a Military Disaster Through Soviet Eyes* (Shepperton: Ian Allan, 1998)

—— and Jonathan M. House *The Battle of Kursk* (Lawrence, KS: University Press of Kansas, 1999)

—— *Zhukov's Greatest Defeat: The Red Army's Epic Disaster in Operation Mars, 1942* (Lawrence, KS: University Press of Kansas, 1999)

—— *Before Stalingrad. Barbarossa – Hitler's Invasion of Russia, 1941* (Stroud: Tempus, 2003)

Grams, Rolf *Die 14. Panzer-Division 1940–1945* (Eggolsheim: Dörfler, n.d.)

Hahn, Fritz *Waffen und Geheimwaffen des deutschen Heeres, 1933–1945* (Bonn: Bernard & Graefe, 1998)

Haupt, Werner *Die Schlachten der Heeresgruppe Süd. Aus der Sicht der Divisionen* (Friedberg: Podzun Pallas, 1985)

Hinze, Rolf *Hitze, Frost und Pulverdampf. Der Schicksalweg der 20. Panzer-Division* (Bochum: Heinrich Pöppinghaus Verlag, 1981)

Hoth, Hermann *Panzer-Operationen. Die Panzergruppe 3 und der operative Gedanke der deutschen Führung Sommer 1941* (Heidelberg: Kurt Vowinckel, 1956)

Jentz, Thomas L. *Panzertruppen 1933–1942. The Complete Guide to the Creation & Combat Employment of Germany's Tank Force. 1943–1945* (Atglen, PA: Schiffer, 1996)

—— *Panzertruppen 1933–1942. The Complete Guide to the Creation & Combat Employment of Germany's Tank Force. 1939–1942* (Atglen, PA: Schiffer, 1998)

Kehrig, Manfred *Stalingrad. Analyse und Dokumentation einer Schlacht* (Stuttgart: Deutsche Verlags-Anstalt, 1979)

Keilig, Wolfgang *Das Deutsche Heer 1939–1945* (Bad Neuheim: Podzun, 1956)

Kirchubel, Robert *Operation Barbarossa 1941. (1) Army Group South* (Oxford: Osprey, 2003)

—— *Operation Barbarossa 1941. (3) Army Group Center* (Oxford: Osprey, 2007)

Klink, Ernst *Das Gesetz des Handelns. Die Operation 'Zitadelle' 1943* (Stuttgart: Deutsche Verlags-Anstalt, 1966)

Lodieu, Didier *III. Pz. Korps at Kursk* (Paris: Histoire & Collections, 2007)

Mackensen, Eberhard von *Vom Bug zum Kaukasus. Das III. Panzerkorps im Feldzug gegen Sowjetrußland 1941/42* (Neckargemünd: Kurt Vowinckel, 1967)

Militärgeschichtliches Forschungsamt (editor) *Das Deutsche Reich und der Zweite Weltkrieg. Band 4: Der Angriff auf die Sowjetunion* (Stuttgart: Deutsche Verlags-Anstalt, 1987)

—— *Band 6: Die Ausweitung zum Weltkrieg und der Wechsel der Initiative, 1941-1943* (Stuttgart: Deutsche Verlags-Anstalt, 1990)

—— *Band 5/I: Organisation und Mobilisierung des deutschen Machtbereichs. Kriegsverwaltung, Wirtschaft und personelle Ressourcen, 1939-1941* (Stuttgart: Deutsche Verlags-Anstalt, 1992)

—— *Band 8: Die Ostfront 1943/44. Der Krieg im Osten und an den Nebenfronten* (Stuttgart: Deutsche Verlags-Anstalt, 2007)

Mitteilungsblatt – Kameradschaft der Wiener Panzer Division, Traditionsgemeinschaft der ehemaligen 2. Panzer Division (various issues in the 1980s, Wien)

Munzel, Oskar *Panzer-Taktik. Raids gepanzerter Verbände im Ostfeldzug, 1941/42* (Neckargemünd: Kurt Vowinckel, 1959)

Niehorster, Leo W. G. *German World War II Organizational Series. Mechanized Army Divisions: 22 June 1941* (Milton Keynes: Military Press, 1994)

—— *Mechanized Army Divisions: 4th July 1943* (Milton Keynes: Military Press, 2004)

—— *Mechanized Army Divisions: 28 June 1942* (Milton Keynes: Military Press, 2005)

Paul, Wolfgang *Brennpunkte – Die Geschichte der 6. Panzer-Division (1. leichte) 1937-1945* (Osnabrück: Biblio Verlag, 1984)

Reinhardt, Klaus *Die Wende vor Moskau. Das Scheitern der Strategie Hitlers im Winter 1941/42* (Stuttgart: Deutsche Verlags-Anstalt, 1972)

Ritgen, Helmut *The 6th Panzer Division 1937-45* (Oxford: Osprey, 1982)

Scheibert, Horst *Entsatzversuch Stalingrad. Dokumentation einer Panzerschlacht in Wort und Bild: Panzer Zwischen Don und Donez. Die Winterkämpfe 1942–1943* (Friedberg: Podzun-Pallas, 1979)

Schicksalweg der 13. Panzer-Division 1939-1945, Der (Eggolsheim: Dörfler, n.d.)

Schneider, Wolfgang *Panzer Tactics. German Small-Unit Armor Tactics in World War II* (Mechanicsburg, PA: Stackpole, 2005)

Senger und Etterlin, Frido von *Die Panzergrenadiere. Geschichte und Gestalt der mechanisierten Infanterie, 1930–1960* (München: J.F. Lehmann Verlag, 1961)

—— *Neither Fear nor Hope. The Wartime Memoirs of the German Defender of Cassino* (London: Greenhill Books, 1989)

—— *Die 24. Panzer-Division 1939–1945. Vormals 1. Kavallerie-Division* (Eggolsheim: Dörfler, n.d.)

Steiger, Rudolf *Panzertaktik im Spiegel deutscher Kriegstagebücher 1939–1941* (Freiburg: Rombach, 1973)

Stolfi, R. H. S. *German Panzers on the Offensive. Russian Front – North Africa, 1941–1942* (Atglen, PA: Schiffer, 2003)

Stoves, Rolf *1. Panzer Division, 1935–1945. Chronik einer der drei Stamm-Divisionen der deutschen Panzerwaffe* (Bad Neuheim: Verlag Hans-Henning – Podzun, 1962)

—— *Die gepanzerten und motorisierten deutschen Grossverbände 1935–1945* (Eggolsheim: Dörfler, 2001)

Strauss, Franz Josef *Die Geschichte der 2. (Wiener) Panzer-Division* (Eggolsheim: Dörfler, n.d.)

Taylor, Brian *Barbarossa to Berlin. A Chronology of the Campaigns on the Eastern Front 1941 to 1945* (Staplehurst: Spellmount, 2003)

Tessin, Georg *Verbände und Truppen der deutschen Wehrmacht und Waffen-SS 1939-1945* (Osnabrück: Biblio, 1977)

Traditionsverband 3. Panzer Division. *Geschichte der 3. Panzer-Division. Berlin-Brandenburg, 1935–1945* (Berlin: Verlag der Buchhandlung Günter Richter, 1967)

Tsouras, Peter G. *Panzers on the Eastern Front. General Erhard Raus and his Panzer Divisions in Russia, 1941–1945* (London: Greenhill, 2006)

Zetterling, Niklas and Anders Frankson *Kursk 1943. A Statistical Analysis* (London – Portland, OR: Frank Cass, 2000)

Ziemke, Earl F. and Magna E. Bauer *Moscow to Stalingrad. Decision in the East* (Washington: U.S. Army Center of Military History, 1968)

—— *Stalingrad to Berlin. The German Defeat in the East* (New York, NY: Military Heritage Press, 1988)

Key to vehicle silhouette identification

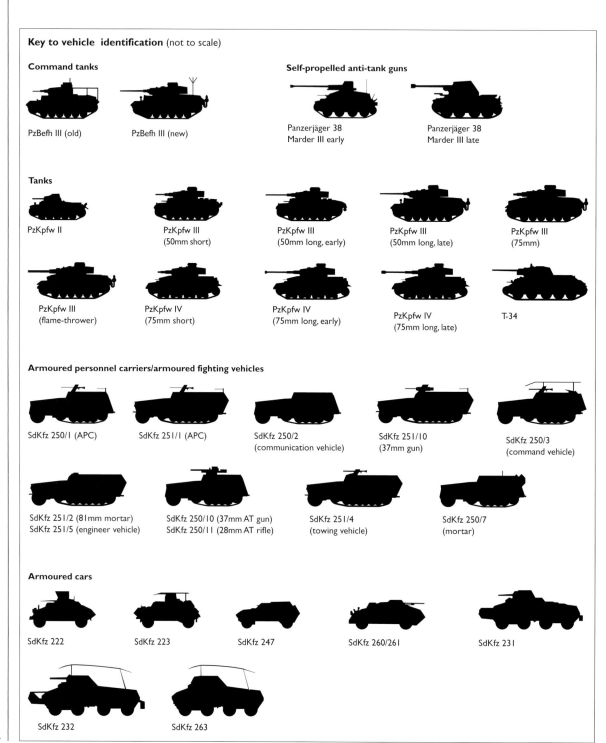

Key to vehicle identification (not to scale)

Command tanks

PzBefh III (old) PzBefh III (new)

Self-propelled anti-tank guns

Panzerjäger 38
Marder III early

Panzerjäger 38
Marder III late

Tanks

PzKpfw II

PzKpfw III
(50mm short)

PzKpfw III
(50mm long, early)

PzKpfw III
(50mm long, late)

PzKpfw III
(75mm)

PzKpfw III
(flame-thrower)

PzKpfw IV
(75mm short)

PzKpfw IV
(75mm long, early)

PzKpfw IV
(75mm long, late)

T-34

Armoured personnel carriers/armoured fighting vehicles

SdKfz 250/1 (APC)

SdKfz 251/1 (APC)

SdKfz 250/2
(communication vehicle)

SdKfz 251/10
(37mm gun)

SdKfz 250/3
(command vehicle)

SdKfz 251/2 (81mm mortar)
SdKfz 251/5 (engineer vehicle)

SdKfz 250/10 (37mm AT gun)
SdKfz 250/11 (28mm AT rifle)

SdKfz 251/4
(towing vehicle)

SdKfz 250/7
(mortar)

Armoured cars

SdKfz 222

SdKfz 223

SdKfz 247

SdKfz 260/261

SdKfz 231

SdKfz 232

SdKfz 263

Index

Figures in **bold** refer to illustrations